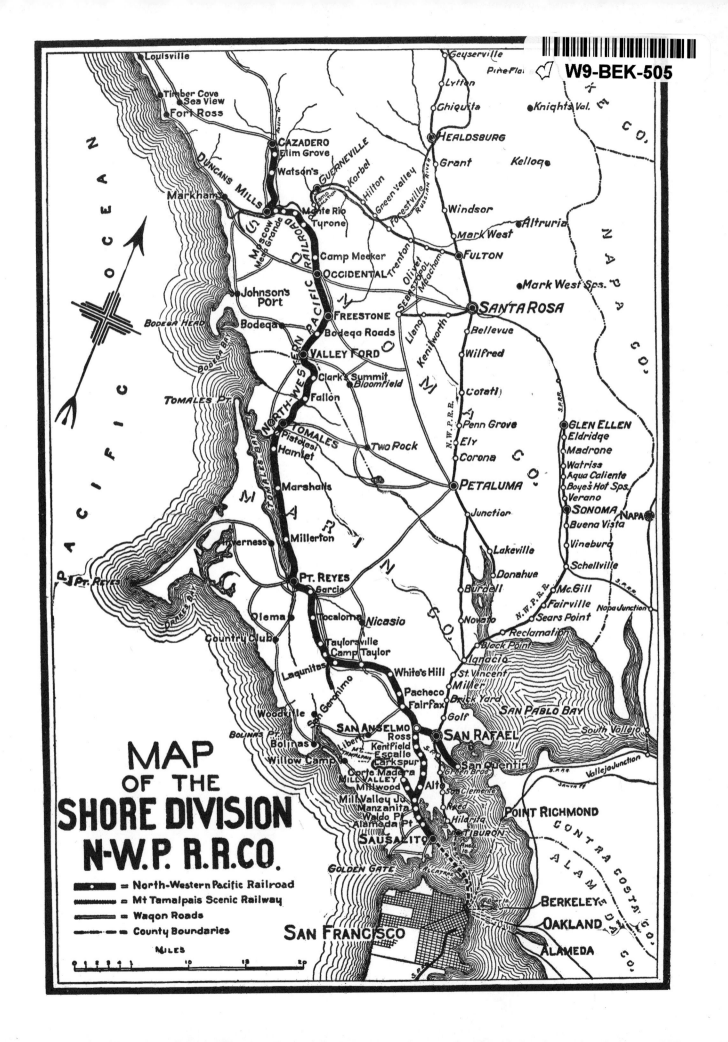

MAP
OF THE
SHORE DIVISION
N-W.P. R.R.CO.

━━━● = North-Western Pacific Railroad
▮▮▮▮ = Mt Tamalpais Scenic Railway
═══ = Wagon Roads
- - - - = County Boundaries

MILES
0 1 2 3 4 5   10   15   20

Sonoma County

The Geysers Hotel at the Geysers in the northeastern corner of Sonoma County; the card was one of a series produced by Northwestern Pacific Railroad promoting tourist spots close to their routes. Courtesy, Mike Capitani

Pictorial Research By
Nancy J. Hutchins

American Historical Press
Sun Valley, California

Sonoma County

T h e   R i v e r   o f   T i m e

An Illustrated History
By Simone Wilson

FRONTISPIECE: Vivid fall colors form a lively mosaic of the wine country and a hop kiln in this painting by Sonoma County artist Frank Gannon. Painted over a 10-year period, this scene captures the essence and feel of the beautifully restored Hop Kiln Winery. Listed with the National Register of Historic Places, the vineyard was the setting for the film Lassie. From the Collection of Cynthia Lee

Page 6/7: One of four wine-growing regions in Sonoma County, the Alexander Valley is home to many wineries. Other regions include Dry Creek, the Russian River, and the Sonoma Valley. Photo by Patty Salkeld

© American Historical Press
All Rights Reserved
Published 1999
Printed in the United States of America

Library of Congress Catalogue Card Number: 99-73749

ISBN: 1-892724-04-9

Bibliography: p. 140
Includes Index

CONTENTS

To my father, Francis Robert Wilson

Anybody can make history. Only a great man can write it.

—Oscar Wilde

Preface

Thomas Hardy once observed that "War makes rattling good history, but Peace makes poor reading." The saga of Sonoma County steers a curse between these two extremes of upheaval and tranquility. Strife and intolerance played their part in the region's history, but so have long intervals of prosperity and growth, when people tended their fields and lived in harmony with their neighbors and the land. Men and women of character established farms and railroads, newspapers and towns, and their personalities shaped the history of the region. Even peace can make good reading.

Sonoma County, blessed with a mild climate and fertile river valleys, attracted waves of immigrants from all directions. The first Americans, crossing from Asia to Alaska, found their way here 5,000 years ago. Russians, Spanish, and Mexicans, extending their empires, met here and vied for control of the coastal lands. Forty-niners hurried to California to mine but stayed to farm. Europeans, Mexicans, and Asians, looking for work and a new life, staked out ranches, built railroads, planted vineyards. All of them left their mark on the county we now call the Redwood Empire, a land touched by beauty and resources. Here is the story of their hopes and endeavors through the years as history—the river of time—flowed through Sonoma County.

Acknowledgments

Any research project is a cooperative effort, and I am indebted to numerous people and organizations for their valuable help: To the Sonoma County Historical Society, especially Glenn Burch, Harry Lapham, John Schubert, and Mary and Adrian Praetzellis, for their cheerful assistance; to Professor Foley Benson of Santa Rosa Junior College, for insight into the life of Native Americans; to Stephen Watrous, professor of history at Sonoma State University, for background on Fort Ross; and to Terry Wright, professor of geology at SSU, for telling me whose fault Sonoma County geology really is. Thanks to Audrey Herman for maintaining a priceless history archive at Sonoma County Library; to Director Eric Nelson and Curator Evangeline Tai of the Sonoma County Museum, to Bo Simons of the Sonoma County Wine Library, and to the West County Museum for their files on filmmaking in western Sonoma County. I am also indebted to the National Maritime Museum and the California Historical Society Library in San Francisco, as well as to all those whose photographs here capture the pulse of life in our region. Thanks also to Hugh Codding for anecdotes on the building boom; to Millie Howie for her expertise on the wine industry; to Mike Capitani for sharing his archives; to Ernestine Smith for memories of postwar Santa Rosa; to Mick Clumpner for enlarging my library, and to Carolyn Martin and the rest of the staff at American Historical Press for their support.

Simone Wilson

This artwork, based upon written reports available in the mid-seventeenth century, depicts Sir Francis Drake being crowned by the American Indians during his brief respite on the coast of California. Courtesy, the Edward Von der Porten Collection

Legacy of the Past

S onoma County, a land of rich valleys, rolling hills, and jagged coast, was born from the rough-and-tumble geologic forces of the Pacific Rim. Sliding continental plates, volcanic effervescence, slow erosion, and coastal uplift all helped shape the coastal ridges, the rugged shore, and the fertile plains. The Pomo Indians, the first inhabitants of northern and central Sonoma County, had their own explanation of the area's formation. In the early time, the earth was perfect. Even the coastline was perfectly straight, because it was made by Marumda the creator and his elder brother Kuksu to a degree of perfection unimagined in the contemporary world. But then Coyote came along and saw the straight coastline and decided that the earth, being perfect, really shouldn't be that way. So he made gigantic waves out on the coastline one day, and they smashed up the entire coastline of Sonoma County. But Coyote made the waves so big that one of them carried him out to sea and nearly drowned him. That's why coyotes don't like water, and that's why Sonoma County has a very rough coastline, because Coyote made it that way.

In another Pomo myth, Marumda and Kuksu were dancing in a sky house. When they were both good and sweaty, Marumda reached under his armpit, scraped out some muck and stuck it between Kuksu's toes. Kuksu did the same to Marumda, and as they danced the land oozed out between their toes.

This primeval tale of muck and motion isn't entirely at odds with the scientific version of geologic events. The bedrock of Sonoma County is the Franciscan formation, formed at the bottom of the Pacific Ocean 100 million years ago. These sediments smashed against the edge of the North American continent, becoming a jumbled mass of muddy sandstone. The dark layers look tumbled and folded, like a pile of wet clothes from the washing machine, maytagged into disarray. Sediments scraped off the floor of the Pacific piled up at the edge of the continent, forming coastal hills. The Russian River held its course as the hills rose, carving a vast watershed.

Other forces were at work along the San Andreas Fault and its branches like the Rodger's Creek Fault that runs directly beneath Santa Rosa and Healdsburg. The faults lend a north-south grain to the landscape. Rocks in fault zones were crushed, making them easy prey to erosion. Broad saltwater bays and lagoons formed in the depressions along the faults, leaving rich deposits. As the water receded, fertile north-south valleys were revealed that would one day nourish vineyards—Sonoma Valley, Alexander Valley, and the Santa Rosa-Cotati plain. Soils around Sebastopol, on the other hand, were laid down by an ancient sea; the resulting sandstone drains easily and makes the hills around Sebastopol ideal for apples.

To the east of the Cotati plain, magma rose to the surface, feeding a chain of volcanic mountains parallel to the coast. Its remnants are the Mayacamas Mountains and Mount Saint Helena, rising 4,344 feet to be the highest point on the eastern skyline. Hot magma is still heating water under the eastern hills. Settlers would build hot spring resorts there, and electric companies would harness escaping steam at the Geysers (which are misnamed—there are no spouting geysers at the Geysers).

With such dramatic geology, Sonoma County was destined to suffer earthquakes. During the 1906 quake the Point Reyes peninsula jumped 17 feet north, and buildings like the Fort Ross Chapel, built right on the fault, collapsed. Loose sediments underlying Santa Rosa shook like jello and devastated the town.

Before people arrived, the elements of future commerce were already in place. Basalt in the hills east of Kenwood would become paving stones in San Francisco. Vast redwood tracts in the northwest would build the city by the bay twice—in the 1800s and again after the 1906 earthquake. Rich soil was waiting for the grapes, apples, prunes, and hops that would nourish the world.

But long before towns, steam plants, and vineyards, the hills and valleys were home to cougar, elk, black tail deer, and the king of California animals, the grizzly that now remains only on the state flag.

Kyrill Khlebnikov, a Russian traveler reporting on the countryside around Fort Ross in the early 1800s, noted that "among quadrupeds the most important are bears, lynx, ordinary wolves, and small ones which the Spaniards call coyotes . . . They catch sturgeon in the Slavianka [Russian] River when the channel is open." Eagles, hawks, ducks, and loons soared over hills laced with redwoods, oak, and alder. Otters, whales, and sea lions swam the coast.

9

People came into this area as long as 5,000 years ago. Siberian parties crossed the land bridge that existed between Asia and Alaska 10,000 years ago during the last ice age. Their descendants gradually filtered down into all corners of the western hemisphere. Coast Miwok, related to tribes in the Sierras and the Central Valley, moved into Marin and southern Sonoma County around Sebastopol, Petaluma, and Bodega Bay. Pomo settled around Clear Lake and then moved southeast, claiming the Russian River drainage as well as the northern Sonoma and southern Mendocino coast. The Wappo lived on the county's eastern edge. The land was dotted with villages, some holding 1,000 people but most only a few dozen.

In their own memory, they had always lived there in the land prepared by the trickster/helper Coyote. According to a Miwok story recorded by Malcolm Margolin, Coyote gathered shiny black raven feathers, and as he walked along he laid a raven feather on top of each hill and named that place. On the following day, humans were living on every hilltop. Coyote told the other animal people, "Now that there is a new people, we will all have to become animals." Immediately all the animal people transformed themselves into birds and mammals and reptiles and insects as Coyote directed.

However they arrived, the first inhabitants gave names to their homes, and some of the names stuck after the Indian presence dwindled. Petaluma means "flat back," a reference to Sonoma Mountain. Cotati is Miwok for "a punch in the face," and Tomales comes from the Miwok for "west."

The Pomo are really six or seven distinct peoples grouped together by Europeans because of linguistic affinity. Pomo of the Russian River barely understood Pomo around Santa Rosa; Pomo languages were as distinct as German, English, and Norwegian. The Miwok spoke a totally different tongue, as different from Pomo as English is from Chinese.

The groups had many customs in common, however. Men stalked elk and deer, the hunter donning a deer skin and antlers and acting deer-like to creep close to his quarry. People went seasonally to streams for salmon and to the shore for mussels, seals, and salt. Women gathered three-quarters of the food, collecting manzanita berries, sap from sugar pines, and edible roots. Acorns from Tanbark oaks and Valley oaks were a prized staple. Women baked acorn meal into bread or cooked it as mush in a watertight basket with a hot rock, stirring occasionally to keep the rock from scorching the basket.

Although white settlers called California Indians "diggers," a derogatory term implying the Indians only ate roots and lived like animals, in fact the north coast Indians lived relatively well without overtaxing themselves or the land. With a warm climate and plentiful resources, the native Pomo, Miwok, and Wappo lived a life of comparative leisure, working only a few hours a day to provide all their needs.

"That left time for basketry, time for prayer, time for nothing at all, time for just being," comments Foley Benson, professor of Native American Studies at Santa Rosa Junior College. "The idea that the hunting and gathering cultures of California were on the verge of starvation, that they lived a bare existence hardly eking out survival, is not true. It's one of the mythologies that we have about them that has no validity."

Leisure time left room for games and artistry. Men played a sport like hockey with a hardwood ball, curved sticks and goal posts. During gambling games, each team sang constantly to distract the other side's players. Children played cat's cradle with string made of plant fiber.

Pomo and Miwok did not make ceramic pots, preferring lightweight watertight baskets for cooking. Pomo women achieved the most sophisticated basketry in North America, a tradition they keep alive today. They collected willow and pulled up long strands of sedge root from sandy stream beds. Some coiled baskets, woven as gifts, were covered in the bright feathers of mallards, meadowlarks, or blue jays, with flourishes of scarlet woodpecker crests. Miniature Pomo baskets, made for healing purposes, are the smallest baskets with designs ever made, ranging in size from two inches to the size of a pinhead.

The Pomo regarded natural resources not as commodities but as partners in harmony with man. They saw the salmon run and the acorn harvest as spiritual powers, and their ceremonies were designed to put man in the

OPPOSITE, TOP: This 1816 drawing illustrates Bay Area natives using a tule reed canoe, which was used to navigate coastal waters. Courtesy, The Bancroft Library

OPPOSITE, BOTTOM: The earliest inhabitants of Sonoma County included tribes such as the Pomo, Wappo, and Miwok, who lived well upon the abundant resources of the land. Courtesy, The Bancroft Library

BELOW: The Pomo kept in balance with nature, taking what they needed and limiting their population. One method of controlling growth may have been the sweat house, a communal lodge where the men lived away from their wives. Courtesy, Peña Adobe Museum

right relation to plants and animals. Without this harmony, the deer and salmon might be offended and remain aloof. The relation between hunter and hunted was one of reciprocal courtesy: The deer allowed itself to be killed; the hunter respected the animal's sacrifice by not wasting anything.

When whites arrived there were perhaps 8,000 Pomo in Sonoma, Lake, and Mendocino counties—not enough to deplete natural resources. Numerous customs kept the population low. Men lived away from their wives in a men's house, a semi-subterranean, communal lodge that served as a sweat house, where the heat of daily sweat baths probably inhibited sperm production.

In addition to the men's house, many communities had a Round House up to 70 feet in diameter for assemblies and ceremonies. Along the coast Pomo built conical dwellings of redwood bark; inland homes were made of grass or tule. The Pomo fashioned strings of shells for currency. Gathering shells from Bodega Bay's clam beds, they cut, drilled, and strung 200 beads at a time. Longer beads made from the thickest part of the shell were more prized, as were older beads polished through a lifetime of handling. Most valuable of all were beads of magnesite ore, which were baked until they changed from dull grey to bright red with colorful bands. Pomos traded these individually or used them as jewels in shell necklaces. By A.D. 1500 they were the prime suppliers of money to peoples farther east.

The first 50 centuries of Sonoma County history passed in relative abundance and isolation, until a day in 1542 when a Pomo on the shore collecting mussels might have looked out to sea, astonished to see a ship heading north. When Europeans discovered the existence of the western hemisphere in 1492, the two dominant sea powers lost no time in staking their claims to the unexplored and possibly lucrative territory. In 1493 Pope Alexander VI, with a stroke of the Papal pen, sliced in two this great terra incognita, with most of the Americas assigned to Spain

and much of Asia to Portugal.

In 1513 Vasco Nuñez de Balboa stood on a hill in Honduras and viewed the Pacific Ocean; by 1520 Hernan Cortez had conquered Mexico and plundered its capital of Tenochtitlan. Rumors of Golden Cities, the so-called Seven Cities of Cibola, sparked land and sea expeditions from Mexico. But Spain sought another prize: a sea route to the Orient through the new lands, one faster and less hazardous than the treacherous passage Magellan found in 1520 at the tip of South America.

Sailors looking for these fabled Straits of Anian were the first Europeans to see the coast of California. Juan Cabrillo, sailing from New Spain (Mexico), cruised north along the coast, stopping at San Diego. Cabrillo died on his flagship, but his pilot Bartolome Ferelo took the ship north to Cape Mendocino, passing the Sonoma coast and surprising any native Americans looking out to sea. The first seafarer to land in the region, however, was the upstart English navigator Francis Drake.

The daring English mariner, with Queen Elizabeth's blessing, sailed from Plymouth in 1577 to plunder the lumbering Spanish galleons in his quick little ship, the *Golden Hinde*. Drake braved the Straits of Magellan and headed north along the Pacific coast, leisurely sacking Spanish ports in Chile and Peru and liberating a fortune in gold from the galleon *Cacafuego*. He then sailed north along the California coast, hoping to discover the legendary straits and scoot back to England.

No straits appeared, so Drake, with a leaky ship and a fabulous cargo, retreated south looking for a harbor to repair the *Golden Hinde*—and keep out of view of the Spanish. In June 1579 he dropped anchor in a sheltered bay and claimed the land for England. The voyagers named it New Albion, because "the white bancks and cliffes, which lie toward the sea" reminded them of their own English coast, wrote Drake's chaplain, Francis Fletcher.

The chaplain's description of the bay is vague, and because Drake's log was lost, no one knows for sure where

the *Golden Hinde* lingered for five weeks in the summer of 1579. Bodega Bay, Drake's Bay in Marin County, and even San Francisco Bay all have their partisans. Today most historians favor Drake's Bay—its white cliffs are the most striking—but Spanish mariners assumed his layover was in Bodega Bay.

Native people, most likely Coast Miwok judging from the few Indian words in Fletcher's memoirs, were fascinated with the white-faced visitors, whom they may have taken for spirits of the dead. The meeting was a friendly one with an exchange of gifts: English linen shirts for local feathers, quivers, and skins. Drake's party judged the Miwok to be a sturdy, good-natured people.

"They are a people of a tractable, free and loving nature, without guile or treachery," Fletcher wrote. "Yet are the men commonly so strong of body, that that which two or three of our men could hardly beare, one of them would take upon his backe, and without grudging carrie it easily away, up hill and downe hill an English mile together."

Drake's crew spent five foggy weeks in the harbor, where they got a taste of typical Sonoma coast summer weather: "During all which time," Fletcher lamented, "notwithstanding it was in the height of Summer, and so

ABOVE: After plundering a fortune from Spanish forts in Chile and Peru, Sir Francis Drake sailed his galleon, the Golden Hinde, *northward, eventually dropping anchor to make repairs in a secluded bay somewhere off the Northern California coast in 1579. Courtesy, Raymond Aker*

OPPOSITE: This engraving by Thomas de Leu depicts explorer Sir Francis Drake, who came ashore in Northern California on June 17, 1579, at the midpoint of his world voyage. The voyage began in November 1577 at Plymouth, England. Although brief, Drake's California sojourn was the first English encampment on the shores of the land that would become the United States. Here the first Protestant church service was held, and first English claim was made to this new land, which Drake named New Albion. Courtesy, Edward Von der Porten Collection

neere the Sunne, yet were wee continually visited with like nipping colds."

The English claim to New Albion was more a cocky gesture to nettle the Spanish than a practical conquest. England lacked the resources to challenge Spain near its Mexican stronghold. But Drake's claim strengthened Spain's resolve to colonize California. Sebastian Vizcaino charted the California coast in 1602, recommending Monterey Bay for an outpost since it was "the best port that could be desired, for besides being sheltered from all the winds, it has many pines for masts." Colonization began only in 1769, when Gaspar de Portola and Franciscan missionary Junipero Serra came north from Mexico. They passed by Monterey, reckoning it could not be the place Vizcaino had so enthusiastically described, and so pressed on to discover San Francisco Bay.

Lieutenant Juan Francisco Bodega y Cuadra, looking for San Francisco Bay after a voyage north in the *Sonora*, blundered into Bodega Bay on October 3, 1775, the first European to come to Sonoma County (with the possible exception of Drake). Indians, paddling out in tule canoes, "most liberally presented us with plumes of feathers, rosaries of bone, garments of feathers . . . " wrote Francisco Mourelle, the *Sonora*'s pilot. As usual, the Indians were welcoming and the weather was not. Fierce tides buffeted the schooner, and its auxiliary boat "was broken into shivers."

Bodega y Cuadra anchored near the mouth of Tomales Bay, which he mistook for the outlet of a river, but his name eventually came to rest on the bay to the north. Later settlers mistakenly assumed the name came from *bodega,* the Spanish word for warehouse, because of a Russian storehouse built there in the early 1800s.

Loss of their landing craft prevented the *Sonora*'s crew from coming ashore, so credit for the first land expedition in Sonoma County goes to a small party of

Spaniards. In 1776 the American Revolution was raging on the east coast, but in California colonization had only just begun. In October, while their colleagues were laying out the new presidio of San Francisco, Lieutenant Fernando Quiros and his pilot Jose Canizares took a small party by boat across San Pablo Bay and meandered up the Petaluma River, believing it would connect with Tomales Bay. They found no passage to the coast but explored the land around Petaluma.

An English captain, James Colnett, took refuge in Bodega Bay in 1790 and charted the area. Evidently he believed this was Drake's haven; Colnett identified his map as "a sketch by compass of Port Sr. Fs. Drake."

By then the Spanish government, seriously alarmed about Russian trappers and about the English at Vancouver, were determined to start an outpost north of San Francisco. Lieutenant Juan Matute came to Bodega Bay in 1794 with orders to start a garrison at the notoriously shallow bay. His ship, the *Sutil,* had a shallow enough draft to enter the harbor, but a follow-up ship from Mexico was too

Ivan Kuskov founded Fort Ross in June 1812 as the first Russian colony in California. The Russian Orthodox Chapel is pictured here. Courtesy, Sonoma County Library

large for the bay and had to return to San Francisco with its troops and supplies. When scouts reported the difficulties of building an overland route to Bodega Bay, the viceroy abandoned plans for the outpost. The coast was clear for the Russians to capitalize on the Spanish failure.

Russia coveted the Pacific Northwest as early as 1741, when the Bering Expedition to Alaska brought back 900 sea otter pelts, prized for their thick warm fur. Russian influence expanded in an arc across the northern Pacific from Kamchatka across to the Aleutians and the Alaskan mainland. Between 1745 and 1800 the lucrative fur trade spawned three dozen trading companies.

But hunters rapidly killed or dispersed the otter herds. By 1797 only a handful of competitors remained. They joined forces and emerged as the Russian-American Company, a private company which nevertheless had major supporters (not to mention stockholders) in the Russian Imperial Court. At its head in Sitka, Alaska, was Alexander Baranov, the kind of tough, independent trader needed to hold together a remote outpost. Baronov was lauded by Washington Irving as "a rough, rugged, hospitable, hard-drinking old Russian, a boon companion of the old roystering school."

As governor of the company from 1799 to 1818, Baranov faced two problems. He calculated the Russians had taken 100,000 otter pelts in the last decade of the century alone; the precious resource was vanishing from Alaskan shores. Also, starvation was a constant threat for the colonists. Alaska's growing season was short. The company's head office noted that "grain brought to the colonies from Siberia via Okhotsk is very expensive, and besides it is subject to loss because of frequent shipwrecks."

Baranov looked south for a solution to his headaches, especially after Count Nicolai Rezanov, a Russian Imperial chamberlain, ignored a Spanish embargo and sailed the *Juno* into San Francisco harbor in 1806. The Spanish, while officially aloof, were only too happy to trade for the *Juno's* supplies—Flemish cloth, axes, sail cloth, and packets of needles. Rezanov in turn loaded up the *Juno* with Spanish wheat, lard, jerky, and garbanzo beans to take north to Sitka. Charming as well as bold, Rezanov cemented the amicable relations with the Spanish by becoming engaged to Maria de la Conception Arguello, the daugh-

Mission San Francisco Solano de Sonoma is shown as it may have looked in the 1820s. The "Great Adobe Church" (built 1827-1832) is believed to have been destroyed by an unexpected rainstorm while its roof was being repaired in 1838. It was replaced by the present building, which was constructed as a parish church by General Mariano Vallejo between 1840 and 1841. Courtesy, California Department of Parks and Recreation and James B. Alexander

ter of the presidio commandant. Rezanov stopped on his way back home to urge Baranov to expand into the unoccupied coast of Northern California. Traveling home through Siberia, he died; the unfortunate Maria waited faithfully for years before learning of his death.

After several successful hunting forays as far south as San Diego, Baranov sent his associate Ivan Kuskov to choose a site for a California colony. In 1809 Kuskov anchored in Bodega Bay, which he called Roumiantzof Bay. He set up a temporary post and explored the Sonoma coast, selecting a coastal bluff 10 miles north of the Russian River. Kuskov returned there in June 1812 on the schooner *Chirikov* with 25 Russians and 80 Aleuts in baidarkas (hunting kayaks) to found the fort of Ross, an archaic name for Russia.

To counter the Russian presence, the Spanish (and, after 1821, the new Mexican Republic) finally extended their influence north of San Francisco. The last mission—San Francisco Solano de Sonoma—went up in 1823, 11 years after the founding of Fort Ross. The Russian empire, moving south, and the Spanish empire, inching northward, came head to head on the soil of Sonoma County.

The Rule Ranch was the residence of Elizabeth Rule, a prominent citizen of Sonoma County in the mid-1800s. From Thompson, Atlas of Sonoma County, California, *1877*

Forts and Haciendas

The Russians and the Spanish—keen rivals if not exactly enemies—were in conflict when Russia established a southern base at Fort Ross on the Sonoma coast. The Spanish and later the Mexicans tried to discourage the Russians by forbidding them to hunt otters and by founding two missions north of San Francisco to block further expansion by the Tsar. On a person-to-person basis, however, relations were much cozier. No sooner was the Russian fort built than mission fathers came around to trade. According to Kyrill Khlebnikov, an officer of the Russian-American Company, "The local Spaniards were at first surprised to see these people, whom they had previously known only by hearsay and who lived in the stormy far off north, so close and so similar to themselves. All during the time the administration was corresponding with the Mexican Viceroy about the situation, the missionaries and other inhabitants became acquainted with their new neighbors and supplied them with livestock, grain and poultry, in defiance of their own government's prohibition of this very thing."

When the Russians first arrived in 1812, however, they were unsure of their reception, so they immediately set to work on a stockade. The redwood fort had two corner blockhouses, each housing half a dozen small cannons. Despite this martial display, an informant for Sonoma's General Mariano Vallejo reported in 1833 that "the walls could not withstand a cannon ball of any calibre," though they would certainly repel an assault with bows and arrows.

In the first few years the colonists built a commandant's house, barracks, and storehouses. They finished the Russian Orthodox chapel in 1824. (Today the restored fort is maintained by the state Department of Parks and Recreation.) Outside the stockade were cattle barns, windmills, a dairy, and two rows of houses with gardens. By the time French diplomat Duflot de Mofras visited in 1840, the fort boasted a high level of culture under its final commandant, Alexander Rotchev, and his accomplished wife, Princess Elena Gagarina. "Anyone who has led the dreary life of a trapper," wrote De Mofras, "or has been pursued by the yells of savages, can fully appreciate the joy of a choice library, French wines, a piano, and a score of Mozart." His reception, he added, was "almost European."

The Russians kept Rumiantsev (Bodega Bay) as their chief port but centered their efforts at the blufftop fort. Father Mariano Payeras, a visitor in 1822, observed a blacksmithy, forge, tannery, and bathhouse along Fort Ross Creek. The bathhouse ran on the same principle as Indian sweat houses; steam rose from hot stones sprinkled with water while the men sat on benches relaxing and swapping stories. "They enter naked and soon begin to sweat oceans," Payeras wrote in his diary.

Ross colonists began the first shipyard in California. Its singular lack of success can be blamed on the shipwrights' unfamiliarity with native wood. Chief carpenter Grudinin built four brigantines, all of improperly seasoned oak. Rot set in just as the ships were launched; within a few years not one was seaworthy. The Russians had better luck making redwood barrels, used for salting away meat and whale oil. The chief business of the outpost, however, was the sea otter hunt. The economy of Russian America was based on fur trade. A dense, glossy, otter pelt brought 40 times the price of a sable fur in the markets of Manchuria, where nobles trimmed their coats with otter fur. Ross's founding party included only 25 Russians; the rest were 80 Aleut Indians from Alaska who hunted in kayaks on the open sea. These "marine cossacks" quickly devastated local otter herds. By 1820 otters were already becoming scarce along the California coast. In 1821 the annual catch had dwindled from hundreds of pelts to only 32.

As the otters disappeared, fort managers turned to agriculture to justify Ross's existence with the Russian-American Company. Kuskov, the first manager, had a passion for gardening, planting pumpkins, squash, and watermelons. He kept Sitka, the capital of Russian America, supplied with pickled beets, and he was probably the first Sonoma County gardener to curse the persistent native gopher.

The colonists imported Sonoma County's first grapevines from Peru in 1817, and they planted hundreds of apple, cherry, and pear trees on slopes behind the fort. They also planted wheat fields near the fort, but, Payeras wrote, "These produce little, and that is of poor quality due to the extraordinary cold and constant fog."

To escape the grey weather, Russians expanded into inland valleys in the 1830s. Khlebnikov Ranch was north of the Estero de Americano, and Kostrominitov Ranch was on Willow Creek. Chernykh Rancho, which may have been near Freestone or Graton, had 2,000 vine stalks in addition to its wheat fields. The Russians were not savvy farmers, however, and never grew enough food to supply the Alaskan colonies.

The Russians hired local Kashaya Pomo to do the actual field work, and Ross became a tricultural society with Russians, Aleuts, and Pomo workers living in mutual tolerance. The Russian contingent included few women, so colonists often married Kashaya women; some of these migrated to Russia with their children when the colony folded. Unlike the Spanish, Russians had no passion for converting Indians to Christianity and showed a real interest in Indian culture. Scientist Ilia Voznesensky made detailed observations of Indian life, collecting baskets and other artifacts. Today Leningrad has the world's largest collection of Pomo and Miwok crafts.

The Russians were equally curious about nature. A Russian expedition of 1816 brought naturalists Adelbert von Chamisso and Johan Eschscholtz to the California coast; Chamisso named a frail orange flower *Eschscholtzia Californica*—the California poppy. Rotchev and Voznesensky explored the Santa Rosa plain and climbed Mount Saint Helena, naming it after the commandant's wife. But Russians weren't the only ones interested in the fertile plains in the shadow of Mount Saint Helena.

Franciscan missionaries, extending the influence of Catholic Spain, settled a strip along the California coast starting in 1769, founding missions roughly a day's journey apart. Military control was centered at four presidios: San Diego, Santa Barbara, Monterey, and San Francisco. Missions were not only churches but agricultural centers, with hundreds or thousands of Indians enlisted to work the fields, either by persuasion or by force. Each mission was supposed to last for 10 years, after which the Indians, schooled in self-sufficiency, would take over. In practice, however, Indians received little training and missions persisted as church-owned centers of entrenched wealth.

England, France, and the United States all showed interest in the Pacific Northwest, and when Russians showed up on the Sonoma coast, Spanish paranoia increased. To secure their claims to land north of the bay, the Spanish founded Mission San Rafael Arcangel (now in the town of San Rafael) in 1817. In 1821 Mexico broke away from Spain and Alta California became a territory of the new Mexican Republic.

California's Mexican Governor Don Louis Arguello was still worrying about Ross when Father Jose Altamira

asked for permission to found a new mission north of the bay. At 36, Altamira was a young go-getter, zealous and impatient with the older priests who ran Mission Dolores in San Francisco. Altamira argued that Dolores should be closed and the Indian converts relocated in a sunnier climate. Arguello and the 1823 Territorial Assembly agreed, and Altamira took a party across the bay, exploring the Petaluma, Suisun, and Napa valleys before deciding on Sonoma Valley with its "permanent springs of sweet water."

The site promised to be an agricultural paradise. "No one can doubt the mildness of the climate of Sonoma after observing the plants, the very tall trees," Altamira wrote in his diary in June 1823. On July 4, 1823, he and his party rose at dawn and blessed a temporary redwood cross. Troops fired off a volley of shots, neophytes sang hymns,

Russia and Spain were in conflict when Russia established a southern base at Fort Ross on the Sonoma coast. The Russians kept Bodega Bay as their chief port but focused their efforts on the blufftop fort, taking advantage of the coastal site. The Russian Orthodox chapel with its two towers is pictured in this photo. Courtesy, Don Silverek Photography

and Altamira celebrated mass in gratitude for the new mission, which he named New San Francisco.

Not everyone was so enthusiastic. Altamira had neglected to ask his Franciscan superiors in San Francisco for permission to trudge off into the hinterlands and start a new mission to replace their own. Altamira's elderly opponents died before they could dislodge him. As a compromise he dropped the "New" and called the Sonoma mission San Francisco Solano, in honor of a Peruvian saint. It was the last and northernmost of California's 21 missions, and the only one founded under Mexican rule.

By 1825 Altamira had a 120-foot-long adobe with a tile roof. Ironically, the Russians were good neighbors, showing up for the dedication of the church in 1824 with altar cloths, candlesticks, mirrors, and a bell. The mission, designed to thwart Russian expansion, led instead to a constant flow of trade between the two remote outposts. Russians bought wheat and cattle from the mission; missionaries came to the Russians for long boats to cross the bay.

Gradually a mission community developed with about 700 Indian residents, mostly transfers from other missions. But the Indian workers revolted against the harsh young priest; he fled to San Rafael and was replaced by Fra Buenaventura Fortuny, who was older and apparently wiser.

General Mariano Vallejo reviews his troops in this view of the north side of the Sonoma Plaza. This painting was made in 1880 from General Vallejo's recollection. Courtesy, California Department of Parks and Recreation and James B. Alexander

Altamira was not alone in being disliked. Most California Indians feared and hated the Spanish. Sonoma coast Indians like the Kashaya Pomo welcomed the Russians as a buffer against them. An anonymous ensign reporting to Mariano Vallejo in 1833 wrote that Miwok Indians around Bodega Bay watched over Russian warehouses there because the Russians in turn protected them from the Spanish. Auguste Duhaut-Cilly, a French sea captain, visited the Solano mission in August 1827 and wrote, "The Spanish government of California has always followed the atrocious system of ordering, from time to time, excursions to the settlements of the interior, either for retaking the Indians escaped from the missions, or driving away los gentiles the [non-missionized Indians] . . . expeditons which, while costing the life of some soldiers and many natives, have served but to nourish hatred."

By the 1830s the mission era was drawing to a close. Californios, the settlers from Spain, were jealous of the missions' huge land holdings. In 1833 Mexico ordered the Franciscans to emancipate the Indians and dissolve the missions. The government dispatched Mariano Guadelupe Vallejo, at age 27 the commandant of the San Francisco Presidio, to take charge of the secularization of Sonoma Mission in 1835. As commanding officer of "La Frontera del Norte" —the northern frontier—Vallejo was ordered to settle the area to assert Mexican claims and thwart the Russians.

Like many Californios who were in the right place at the right time, Vallejo benefitted immensely from the breakup of the mission system. His ranches absorbed livestock and Indian laborers from the San Rafael and Sonoma missions. Vallejo's mandate in the north included settlement of the region, and under his direction Sonoma County's richest land was parceled out as ranchos, chiefly to members of his own extended family, which was considerable.

Most of California's arable land was divided into 800 ranchos, most of them granted by the Mexican government between 1823 and 1846. At 66,000 acres, Vallejo's Petaluma Rancho was one of the biggest in the state. Ranchos were devoted not to crops but to cattle raised for hides; this was the colorful era of the mounted vaquero ruling vast grazing lands. Property rights were relaxed in the extreme, as noted by John Bidwell, an early American immigrant: "When you wanted a horse to ride, you would take it to the next ranch—it might be 20, 30 or 50 miles—and turn it out there, and sometime or other in reclaiming his stock the owner would get it back. In this way you might travel from one end of California to the other." A hungry traveler was allowed to kill and eat another man's cows as long as he left the hides hanging with the brand in plain sight.

The northern frontier was a wilderness; Vallejo had to persuade fellow Californios to come and apply for vast tracts of land. He convinced his widowed mother-in-law, Doña Maria Carrillo, to come north. Doña Maria packed seven Spanish trunks with her finery, assembled the nine

Carrillo children who still lived with her (three older daughters were already married), and headed north along El Camino Real to stay with her daughter Benecia, Vallejo's wife. After a brief stay in Sonoma, she moved over the hill to Santa Rosa Creek in 1837 and built the Carrillo adobe, the first European home in the Santa Rosa Valley.

Yankee sea captains, sailing between California and Peru, lived among the Californios and courted the much younger daughters of prosperous families. A handful married into the sprawling Carrillo/Vallejo family and applied for their own ranchos. Scottish sea Captain John Wilson married Benecia's sister, Ramona Carrillo, and received Los Guilucos Rancho (including present-day Kenwood) in 1837. Captain John Rogers Cooper, married to Vallejo's sister Encarnacion, took 18,000-acre El Molino Rancho (present-day Forestville) in 1836 and built the state's first power sawmill there. Captain Henry Fitch, who eloped with Benecia's sister, got the Sotoyome grant (now Healdsburg) in 1840. Fitch looked after trade in San Diego and sent Cyrus Alexander to develop the rancho, promising him 10,000 acres in return. Alexander picked the choice Alexander Valley as his payment and moved there. Merchant Jacob Leese wed Rosalia, yet another sister of Vallejo, and received the Huichica Rancho east of Sonoma.

Other ranchos went to members of the Carrillo family. In Santa Rosa Valley, Matriarch Doña Maria had the 8,800-acre Cabeza de Santa Rosa Rancho, so named because the home lay at the head (cabeza) of the creek. Her eldest son Joaquin received the 13,000-acre Llano de Santa Rosa Rancho (Sebastopol and the Laguna area); he built a home west of the Laguna and later started a hotel. British travel writer Frank Marryat, visiting the county in 1850, saw Doña Maria's son Ramon, then in his 20s, as the quintessential Californio:

Don Raymond was a striking-looking fellow, well built and muscular, with regular features, half concealed by his long black hair and beard. The loose Spanish dress, the heavy iron spurs, the lasso hanging from the saddle, and the gaunt but fiery colt on which he was mounted, were all for work and little for show . . .

Mariano Vallejo himself built a two-story building (now preserved as the Petaluma Adobe) at his vast rancho in the Petaluma Valley. The adobe was the center of a flourishing rancho, with a tannery and blacksmith shop that turned out saddles, bridles, and spurs for Vallejo's horsemen. Indian workers filled his warehouses with corn and wheat.

But Vallejo was no mere rancher. One of the cultured power-brokers of Mexican California, he absorbed books much the way he absorbed the assets of the missions. The core of Vallejo's collection came from a German merchant who landed in 1831 with a consignment of books. The 200 volumes, some of them on the church's list of forbidden books, were in danger of being confiscated when Vallejo stepped in and acquired them for a good price.

Some ranchos went to people outside the Vallejo family. Jose Berryessa, Vallejo's sergeant, received Rancho Mallacomes (or Mayacamas), a 12,000-acre spread east of present-day Healdsburg. Swiss surveyer Jean Vioget took 23,000-acre Blucher Rancho west of present-day Sebastopol in exchange for surveying other land grants. Vioget had served under German General Blucher against Napoleon at Waterloo. William Mark West, at San Miguel Rancho between El Molino and Cabeza de Santa Rosa, was a ship's carpenter who built roofs for his neighbors' new homes.

Russia monopolized the Sonoma coast, but Vallejo persuaded three Anglo seafarers to develop a rancho just south of the Russian holdings. James Dawson, James Black, and Edward McIntosh settled the Rancho Estero Americano, named after the estuary between Marin and Sonoma counties. McIntosh built the ranch house, destined to be the focus of the strangest dispute in Sonoma County real estate.

ABOVE: *General Mariano Vallejo granted vast acreage to family and friends, including his mother-in-law, Doña Maria Carrillo, who built the Carrillo adobe in 1837. Members of the Carrillo family are pictured in this 1880 photograph. Standing are Nancy, Manuel, Albert, Eli, Mariano Avelardo, and Emma; seated in the front row are John, Marta, Benicia, Joaquin, Rosario, and, in front, Anita. Courtesy, Burton Travis Collection.*

OPPOSITE, TOP: *General Mariano Vallejo was charged with attracting new settlers to Northern California during the rancho era to assert Mexican claims. He divided up vast tracts of land that were to become the backbone of California under Mexican rule. From Thompson,* Atlas of Sonoma County, California, *1877*

OPPOSITE, BOTTOM: *Cyrus Alexander earned part of the Sotoyome grant when he helped Henry Fitch, one of Mariano Vallejo's brothers-in-law, develop his rancho. Alexander took the beautiful Alexander Valley as his payment. From Thompson,* Atlas of Sonoma County, California, *1877*

McIntosh went down to Monterey alone to apply for the rancho in 1839, conveniently leaving Dawson's name off the grant application. Dawson, who signed papers with an "X" anyway, didn't discover the deception until 1843. In a rage Dawson sawed the house in two and hauled his half across the property line, applying for neighboring Rancho Pogolimi. Dawson's widow later married Frederick Blume (from which the name Bloomfield probably comes).

In 1839 the Russian-American Company added up accounts and decided the Ross colony was a lost cause. Hedged in by Mexican ranchos, the Russians could not expand the farms enough to turn a profit. Alexander Rotchev negotiated a deal in 1841 with Captain John Sutter, a powerful merchant in the Sacramento Valley. Sutter offered $30,000 for the fort's moveable assets—the proverbial lock, stock, and barrel. After a stay of 39 years on the Sonoma coast, the Russians sailed for home. The Ross colony never numbered more than 500, including about 100 Russians, but its importance was greater than its size. It marked the farthest eastward extent of Imperial Russia and spurred corresponding expansion by the Spanish and Mexicans.

Sutter sent his agent John Bidwell to Fort Ross to send along anything valuable, including, wrote Bidwell, "forty-odd pieces of old rusty cannon and one or two small

ABOVE AND FACING PAGE, BOTTOM: After withdrawal of Russian traders from Bodega Bay in 1841, Mexican and American rivalry in the region increased. In 1846 agitation for incorporation within the United States culminated in a revolt, supported by John C. Frémont, above, an American officer engaged at the time in an exploring expedition. A group of 20 settlers left Frémont's camp at Sutter's Fort on June 11, 1846. Disenchanted with Mexican rule, they mounted a rebellion known as the Bear Flag Revolt. Peter Storm, who is believed to be the creator, is shown here with the original Bear Flag. Courtesy, Napa County Historical Society; Frémont courtesy, Vacaville Heritage Council

OPPOSITE, TOP: Although the basic structure of La Casa Grande, the residence of General Mariano Vallejo, may be accurately depicted, this watercolor shows ornate detailing that probably never existed on the actual building. La Casa Grande was destroyed in an 1867 fire. Courtesy, The Bancroft Library and James B. Alexander

brass pieces, with a quantity of old French flintlock muskets, pronounced by Sutter to be of those lost by Bonaparte in 1812 in his disastrous retreat from Moscow." Bidwell spent a year at the fort, boxing up muskets and making cider from apples left behind in the Russian orchard.

With the Russians gone, the coast was clear for new settlers to move into their old haunts. German immigrants Charles Meyer and Ernest Rufus claimed the coastal strip north of the Russian River, acquiring the 18,000-acre German Rancho in 1846.

Yet another sea captain, 61-year-old Stephen Smith, took the coast south of the Russian River, settling on the

35,000-acre Bodega Rancho in 1840 with his 16-year-old Peruvian bride, Manuella Torres. The enterprising Yankee captain imported machinery for the state's first steam-powered lumber and flour mill. He also added a little culture to California, bringing three pianos around the Horn, one of which took center stage in Vallejo's parlor.

No sooner had the Russians packed up and left than a far greater invasion threatened from the east: American settlers, inspired by the accounts of mountain men like Jedediah Smith, began to trickle over the Sierras, looking for the fertile valleys of California. The first organized group was the Bartleston-Bidwell party from Missouri (the same Bidwell that John Sutter later sent to Ross). The bedraggled pioneers reached the haven of Sutter's New Helvetia settlement in 1842, followed by several hundred land-hungry settlers who moved into the Sacramento, Sonoma, and Napa valleys, much to the dismay of the Mexican government. Two Donner children, survivors of the ill-fated party trapped by Sierra snows, found a haven with settlers in Sonoma.

General Vallejo, by now one of the premier statesmen of Mexican California, was tolerant of Anglos, especially with so many in his own family. Nevertheless, by 1845 Vallejo and his compatriots feared their homeland would be overrun. "The emigration of North Americans to California today forms an unbroken line of wagons from the United States clear to this Department," Vallejo wrote. "I see with regret what I predicted to the National Government more than eight years ago gradually coming true. The stream of Americans then was only considerable, and today it is frightful."

Distrust increased between Americans and Californios, fueling rumors that Mexico would expel the pioneers. In 1846 a U.S. naval contingent was poised near the port of Monterey, hoping for an excuse to annex California. American scout John C. Frémont and his band were waiting in the hills, encouraging rebellion. In June a rumor swept the pioneer community that Mexico had ordered all Americans to quit California and retrace their steps across the Sierras. In protest a party of outraged farmers, mostly from Napa and Sacramento, rode off to capture Sonoma, staging the greatest comic opera of nineteenth-century California: the Bear Flag Revolt.

Sonoma was a pueblo with few soldiers when the 33 Bear Flaggers rode up at daybreak on June 14, 1846. They were a scruffy and varied bunch as they surrounded Vallejo's Sonoma home. "Some wore the relics of their homespun garments, some relied upon the antelope and the

bear for their wardrobe," wrote one of the party. "There was the grim old hunter with his long heavy rifle, the farmer with his double-barreled shotgun . . . others with horse-pistols, revolvers, sabres, ships cutlasses, Bowie knives." Ezekiel "Stuttering" Merritt, captain of the impromptu band, and several others disappeared inside the house to talk terms with Vallejo, who generously opened up his supply of brandy. After several hours, the remaining party outside got restless and chose a captain to investigate. He did not reappear either. Finally William Ide, another of the band, slipped inside to discover the delay.

"There sat Merritt—his head fallen," wrote Ide, ". . . and there sat the new made Captain as mute as the seat he sat upon. The bottles had well nigh vanquished the captors." The Bear Flag party pulled itself together long enough to declare a revolutionary Bear Flag Republic, taking Vallejo and a few relatives hostage and hustling them off to Sutter's Fort in Sacramento, where they remained prisoners for several months. The Bears then improvised a banner "made of plain cotton cloth, and ornamented with the red flannel of a shirt from the back of one of the men," wrote Ide. The flag bore the words "California Republic" and the image of a grizzly bear, symbolizing "strength and unyielding resistence," added Ide. The Bears were not artists; onlookers reported the celebrated bear looked more like a prize porker.

The episode turned tragic when two Bears, Thomas Cowie and George Fowler, rode toward Fitch Rancho for spare ammunition. A party of Californio *defensores* waylaid the pair north of the Carrillo adobe and killed them. An avenging group of Bears, led by Frémont and Kit Carson, chased the Californio party, which escaped across the bay. Near San Rafael the Bears captured three non-combatants, Jose Berryessa and two teenaged brothers named de Haro. According to Carson's account, Frémont told Carson he "had no room for prisoners, but do your duty," whereupon Carson shot all three. The violent exchange left a legacy of bitterness between Mexicans and Yankees, an unnecessary one since many Californios, Vallejo among them, were by then resigned to the U.S. annexation.

The grizzly banner flew over Sonoma for 22 days. Word of the Mexican-American War then reached California, and the Bear revolt was absorbed into the greater conflict. The Bears had jumped the gun on history. Mexico lost the war and in 1848 ceded California to the United States. The Mexican era was at an end. Ahead were gold and statehood.

*A brass band and a crowd of citizens turned out to greet the train in this 1887
photo taken in Guerneville. Courtesy, Sonoma County Library*

CHAPTER THREE

Building Main Street

The 1850s were a crucial decade that saw the breakup of vast ranchos and the beginning of towns in Sonoma County. With the advent of the Mexican War, the town of Sonoma came under several years of military rule. Sonoma housed regular troops as well as Companies C and H of Stevenson's Regiment, a special unit recruited to strengthen the U.S. hold on California. Colonel Jonathan Stevenson's New York volunteers—doctors, lawyers, surveyors, mechanics—were chosen for professional skills rather than fighting ability. Some had artistic leanings. Lieutenant George Derby, writing under the name Squibob, penned humorous tales of Sonoma County life. The soldiers formed a theatrical company, enlisting their buddies to play the parts. The regiment staged bear fights, played billiards in General Vallejo's Casa de Billardo on the plaza, and livened up the town.

Mariano Vallejo himself had surveyed Sonoma in the 1830s, laying out a large town square surrounded by lots. By the late 1840s Sonoma's square was an animated but neglected place. Enterprising workmen dug up adobe for bricks and left yawning holes. In one spot a ditch ran through the plaza with a cannon wheel over it as a makeshift bridge. Stevenson's boys and their Californio friends took turns breaking wild horses in the square, in between cockfights and horse races.

The military occupation brought to Sonoma officers like Joseph Hooker and William T. Sherman, who would later distinguish themselves in the Civil War. A veteran of Mexican campaigns, Hooker bought 500 acres in the Valley of the Moon with visions of being a country squire, but when the Civil War broke out he headed east. Wangling an appointment with President Lincoln, Hooker modestly told him, "I was at Bull Run the other day, Mr. President, and it is no vanity in me to say that I am a damned sight better general than any you had on that field." Despite his egotism, Hooker became a favorite of Lincoln's; the president eventually promoted him to commander of the Army of the Potomac.

In February 1848 John Sutter wrote to Vallejo of a gold discovery in the Sierra foothills. Two weeks later Sutter was paying off his debts in Sonoma with samples of gold dust. The gold rush, which brought 100,000 newcomers to California, had the opposite effect on Sonoma.

Within weeks the town was practically empty. A French consul on the scene wrote of Sonoma: "Most of its houses are empty, all work has stopped, and there as everywhere else, there is not a single carpenter left nor a joiner, nor a blacksmith nor any laborer doing the least work. All have gone to the Placer, or have come back from there too rich and too independent to resume their trades . . ."

Townsmen and soldiers alike left Sonoma for the hills. Surveyor Jasper O'Farrell put down his compass and headed for gold country with Jacob Leese, coming home with a tidy profit. Stevenson's boys forgot their regimental duties and followed close behind. Storeowners like Lilburn Boggs did a brisk trade supplying miners until boats took miners directly up the Sacramento River, bypassing Sonoma. The gold rush was in full swing by 1849, giving its name to the 49ers who hastened to California by three routes. Some sailed 18,000 miles around Cape Horn; others shipped to Panama, crossed the isthmus, and came up the coast by paddle-wheel steamer. The majority, especially those from the Ohio and Mississippi valleys, came overland on the California Trail in mile-long wagon trains.

Some who left Sonoma limped back with empty pockets; others returned with fortunes in gold. Helpers at the Blue Wing, a popular tavern and gambling hall, supplemented their income sweeping gold dust off the barroom floor. Dozens of Stevenson's men got discharges and came back to Sonoma, where their qualifications for the regiment also made them admirable townsfolk. Captain John Frisbie, once the commander of H Company, came home to marry one of Vallejo's daughters and open a store in his father-in-law's Casa Grande. A.J. Cox started the county's first newspaper, the *Sonoma Bulletin,* in 1852. C Company's Captain John Brackett represented Sonoma in the first legislature that convened after California became a state in 1850.

Not everyone came to California for gold. Baron Agostin Haraszthy, a Hungarian aristocrat, saw Sonoma Valley as the perfect setting for wine grapes. Political turmoil in Europe drove him to America in 1840, where he pursued a varied career—farming in Wisconsin, publishing tales of his travels, and finally trekking west on the Santa Fe Trail. His California career was equally diverse: he was sheriff in San Diego and later an official of the San

Francisco mint. Vallejo invited Haraszthy to Sonoma in 1856, where he recognized an untapped potential for grapes. "The production is fabulous," Haraszthy wrote in *Grape Culture, Wine and Wine-Making,* "and there is no doubt in my mind that before long there will be localities discovered which will furnish as noble wines as Hungary, Spain, France, or Germany ever have produced." After Haraszthy proved grapes could prosper without irrigation, he went on a state-sponsored tour of Europe in 1861, returning with 300 varieties that became the foundation of Sonoma County's vast wine industry. He planted 6,000 acres of vineyards and founded the Buena Vista Viticultural Socety. Jacob Gundlach and other Sonoma growers came to him for cuttings, and so did vintners from other parts of the state, creating, says local historian Ernest Finley, a "grape rush." Haraszthy and Vallejo competed for wine ribbons at the state fair, but the rivalry was a friendly one: in 1863 Haraszthy's sons Arpad and Attila married Vallejo's daughters Natalie and Jovita. Setbacks in the 1860s prompted Haraszthy to pursue business ventures in Central America, where his death was as colorful as his life. The father of Sonoma County winemaking lost his life crossing a river in Nicaragua; some accounts conclude he was devoured by a alligator.

Meanwhile, the gold rush sparked a town in southern Sonoma County. In 1849, 40,000 new people surged into a state unprepared to feed them; by 1852, 60,000

more had followed. The Petaluma Valley was a paradise of game that drew hunters up the winding Petaluma River. Hunting was a lucrative profession: deer fetched $20 a head in San Francisco markets; quail were $9 a dozen. Two hunters, Tom Baylis and Dave Flogsdel, each put up a trading post at the upper reaches of the river. Baylis later built a warehouse and the Pioneer Hotel, running his own sloop to and from San Francisco. James Hudspeth opened a warehouse at the foot of Washington Street when he discovered he could ship Bodega potatoes cheaper from Petaluma than from Bodega Bay. Meat, wheat, and produce flowed from Sonoma County valleys to the Petaluma wharf, going by boat across the bay to San Francisco or up the Sacramento River. The steamer *Petaluma* embarked on its shake-down cruise in October 1857, chugging down the creek and across to Benecia. The *Sonoma Democrat* reported "some little roughness in her machinery, incident to all new engines," but otherwise it was a successful maiden voyage.

By 1852 the town was taking shape. Mail came on horseback once a week from Benecia. Garrett Keller claimed 158 acres of future downtown Petaluma, and

In 1849 James Cooper and Thomas Spriggs, the latter a ship's carpenter, enlarged this old Sonoma building to its present form and began operating it as a combined hotel, restaurant, and casino. Known as the Blue Wing Hotel, it was a popular gathering place for many early Californians. Courtesy, James B. Alexander

though his legal title was in doubt, buyers confidently purchased the $10 lots and Petaluma grew quickly. In 1855 there were 481 voters; the next year 801. Petaluma's first newspaper, the *Sonoma County Journal,* began in 1855; the *Argus* closely followed and the two merged in the 1860s. Between 1854 and 1860 Petaluma grew faster than any other town in the county, outstripping Sonoma. "The place already contains 2,500 inhabitants, and the air of business and prosperity which it wears is quite striking," wrote New York reporter Bayard Taylor in 1859. Petaluma did not, however, get the coveted status of county seat, an honor which went instead to Santa Rosa.

The nucleus of early activity in Santa Rosa Valley was Doña Maria Carrillo's adobe ranchhouse. David Mallagh, husband of Doña Maria's daughter Juana, and his partner Donald McDonald ran a hotel and store there for traders taking freight by mule to Clear Lake and the Russian River. In 1852 they sold the business to Alonzo Meacham, who in turn sold out to Feodor Hahman, Berthold "Barney" Hoen, and William Hartman, three Germans destined to be movers and shakers in the valley. Soon Hoen and company also bought 70 acres of future downtown Santa Rosa for $1,600 and surveyed the land for a town. Lots went for $25 each. Julio Carrillo's house was the first in the area, built a year before the survey. The first streets bore number and letter names, but later developers didn't follow this simple scheme. The most colorful sequence of street names is described by turn-of-the-century historian Tom Gregory: "An addition was attached to the city by a Mr. Pipher, who had learned to play football at Palo Alto, and the streets of the tract bore the academic legend 'Leland-Stanford-Junior-University,' names fully as unique and as inappropriate for the purpose as would be 'In-God-We-Trust-All-Others-Cash.'"

Franklin Town, on the north bank of Santa Rosa Creek, was an early rival of Santa Rosa. French-Canadian Oliver Beaulieu (variously spelled Bolio, Boileau, etc.) surveyed the town in 1853; John Ball built a small hotel and store there. Franklin's Baptist Church was the first church

The rivalry between Sonoma and fledgling Santa Rosa for the county seat was a hot issue during the state assembly elections of 1853. In September 1854, 716 voted for Santa Rosa as opposed to 563 for Sonoma, thus securing Santa Rosa as county seat. Pictured here is the courthouse in Santa Rosa as it appeared around 1895. Courtesy, Don Silverek Photography

in the valley. The creekside town was Santa Rosa's twin until the celebrated caper of the county seat.

Sonoma, being the only town in the district, was named county seat when the legislature established counties after statehood in 1850. (Sonoma County also included present-day Mendocino County until 1859.) Rivalry between Sonoma and fledgling Santa Rosa was a hot issue in 1854, when State Assemblyman James Bennett of Santa Rosa introduced a bill to let Sonoma County voters choose their county seat. Santa Rosa boosters Barney Hoen and Julio Carrillo pledged to donate land for a new courthouse. Even the *Sonoma Bulletin* admitted the Sonoma courthouse had its failings, noting that officials ran "the risk of being crushed beneath a mass of mud and shingles, for we really believe it will cave in the next heavy rain."

To impress voters with the splendor of Santa Rosa, town fathers held a Fourth of July barbecue and fed everyone within voting distance—about 500 citizens. The shindig had the desired effect: In September 1854, 716

ABOVE AND LEFT: By the time A.W. Russell launched Santa Rosa's first newspaper, the Sonoma Democrat, *on October 22, 1857, Santa Rosa had grown to 100 buildings. By the end of the decade it had 400 citizens and a host of thriving businesses fronting the plaza. Courtesy, Don Silverek Photography*

voted for Santa Rosa versus 563 for Sonoma. Santa Rosans feared Sonomans would not lightly surrender their court records. Slow-moving bureaucracy was not the Santa Rosa style in those days. Following the vote Jim Williamson hitched two mules to a wagon and in the company of county clerk N. M. Menefee rode into Sonoma, loaded up the dusty documents and took off for Santa Rosa 22 miles away. The one-legged Menefee sat beside Williamson, occasionally prodding one of the mules with the end of his peg leg. In this fashion the county records entered the new county seat full tilt. Williamson's charge for the 100-minute freight run was $15.

After the hijacking, A.J. Cox, the wry voice of the *Sonoma Bulletin*, remarked,

We are only sorry they did not take the adobe courthouse along—not because it would be an ornament to Santa Rosa, but because its removal would have embellished our plaza.

Alas 'old casa de adobe.' No more do we see county lawyers and loafers in general, lazily engaged in the laudable effort of whittling asunder the veranda posts—which, by the way, require but little more cutting to bring the whole dilapidated fabric to the ground.

Santa Rosa's elevation to county seat was the death knell for nearby Franklin Town. John Ball and his neighbors moved the mile and a half down the creek to the new town, never dreaming twentieth-century Santa Rosa would expand to include their old haunts.

By the time A.W. Russell launched Santa Rosa's first newspaper, the *Sonoma Democrat,* on October 22, 1857, Santa Rosa had grown to 100 buildings. By the end of the decade it had 400 citizens and a host of thriving businesses fronting the plaza. Williamson's California Livery Stable competed with the Union Livery Stable, once owned by Julio Carrillo. Santa Rosa Bakery sold loaves three for a quarter. Jason Miller's ad for his dry goods store boasted it was in "the fire-proof brick store" in the plaza's southwest corner, a sign that wooden buildings stood in jeopardy from sudden fires. On the opposite corner Henry Moller's Liquor and Oyster Saloon served fresh oysters all night. The Santa Rosa Shaving Saloon handled laundry and baths (10 baths for $4). The Eureka Hotel boasted a bar and billiards, and E.P. Colgan's Santa Rosa House offered stage connections to Petaluma, the Russian River, Sonoma, and the Geysers.

Farther north on the road to Mendocino, Harmon Heald settled on the Sotoyome Rancho in 1850 and claimed land for a town site. Heald surveyed the town in 1857 and sold lots for $15 apiece, setting aside parcels for a school, cemetery, plaza, and churches. By the end of the decade Healdsburg had 500 people and 120 houses. Satirist A. J. Cox had folded his *Sonoma Bulletin* in 1855, announcing to his loyal readers that "the Blunderbuss has dried up." In 1860, however, he turned up as editor of the fledgling *Review,* one of several papers destined to cover Healdsburg news.

More towns emerged farther north. Colonel A.C. Godwin started a store in 1854 that was the nucleus of Geyserville. R.B. Markle bought 800 acres of land near the present Mendocino border. Levi Rosenberg and the Hahman/Hartman team opened stores, while Markle ran a tavern for thirsty pack-train drivers. This stop evolved into

Healdsburg owes its beginnings to Harmon G. Heald, who settled part of the Sotoyome Rancho in 1850. Heald platted the townsite in 1857, including areas designated for a school, churches, a plaza, and a cemetery. By 1860 Healdsburg boasted 120 homes and 500 residents. From Thompson, Atlas of Sonoma County, California, *1887*

Cloverdale. Windsor also started in the mid-1850s with a store and public house; a district of the present town bore the unfortunate name Poor Man's Flat. West county mill towns—Guerneville, Cazadero, Duncans Mills—trace their roots to these early times but did not come into their own until the coming of the railroads.

Joaquin Carrillo was the first Sebastopol resident, building his adobe house on his Llano de Santa Rosa Rancho in 1846. Around the same time James Miller and John Walker founded a store a mile south of the present town. J.H.P. Morris started a rival grocery and saloon, calling his center Pine Grove. Surveyor Jasper O'Farrel named the district Analy (for his sister Ann) when townships were established in the 1860s, but a fistfight in 1856 provided the lasting name for the town. Hibbs, one of the combatants, had retreated into Dougherty's store in Pine Grove. Hibbs wouldn't come out and Dougherty prevented his attackers from coming in. Onlookers compared this local battle to the siege of Sebastopol then going on in the Crimean War.

When California became a territory of the United States, land-hungry pioneers poured in to stake out homesteads in the Golden State's fertile valleys. Gold fever drew thousands more farmers who scouted around for land when their get-rich schemes fell through. Most found themselves in a prolonged legal limbo in which they could neither buy land nor verify who really owned it.

The Treaty of Guadalupe Hidalgo, ending the Mexican-American War in 1848, upheld the property rights of former Mexican citizens. In 1851 the U.S. Congress set up a land commission to verify California land claims. Rancho owners hunted through forgotten trunks for documents proving the boundaries of their land. The commission rejected nearly 200 claims, which then were open to homesteaders. Over 600 claims were confirmed, but only after lengthy appeals by government attorneys. It took an average of 17 years to confirm a land grant; most owners had to break up their huge holdings because they were bankrupt when they finally established title. Mariano Vallejo, for instance, received 44,000 acres of his original 66,000-acre claim, but the financial strain forced him to sell his Petaluma adobe and surrounding land to settlers.

The commission threw out some imaginative claims. Jose Yves Limantour, a French merchant working in Mexico, claimed Sonoma's mission vineyards as well as half of San Francisco and the islands of Alcatraz, Yerba Buena, and the Farallones. U.S. attorneys claimed the signature on Limantour's grant was not that of the Mexican governor, though it did resemble the handwriting of Limantour's secretary. Limantour reaped a quarter of a million dollars from gullible buyers before the federal government threw out his claim. By then he had taken his movable assets back to Mexico.

American farmers, accustomed to homesteading on open land, were dismayed to find all the best land already claimed. Most farmers squatted, hoping the land would become public if the claim were rejected. No one wanted to make improvements to land belonging to someone else, so the first homes were makeshift shanties made of posts and split redwood. In the 1850s these "bachelor ranchos"

Although Paul Hahman's Santa Rosa apothecary business was destroyed in the 1906 earthquake, his ledger shows business as usual resumed just two days later. The drugstore, which is shown as it looked in 1890, had the first plate glass window in Santa Rosa's new downtown. Courtesy, Sonoma County Library

gave way to established farms as families moved in. Settlers clustered at Green Valley, Bodega, Santa Rosa Creek, Dry Creek, and the Russian River Valley, hoping Mexican grants would be tossed out.

In many ways Eliza and James Gregson were typical of these early pioneers. In their early 20s the Gregsons left Illinois with Eliza's mother and two brothers and crossed the plains with ox teams. The exhausted party arrived at Sutter's Fort in 1846, where James worked as a blacksmith and also helped guard the Vallejo party during the Bear Flag Revolt. The Gregsons were the first to settle in Green Valley near Sebastopol, squatting on a 160-parcel they later purchased.

A pioneer with the instincts of a historian, Eliza Gregson wrote her memoirs on the backs of old letters, leaving a rare account of daily life around 1850. She describes tending survivors of the Donner party and seeing glimpses of the first gold dust from Sutter's Mill. She recalls (without much punctuation) the valley when it was virgin land: "when we came to green valley it seemed almost like a paradise . . . grass and clover and flowers in abundance the grass was as tall as myself." Eliza was a witness to the settlement of valleys and the founding of towns like Healdsburg and Sebastopol, while farmers organized county fairs and built better houses, "Leaveing old cabbins to be used for outhouses."

By the time rancho owners proved their claims, dozens of squatters had put down roots. Some formed Squatters Leagues and fought eviction, especially when rancho owners refused to lease or sell. There was bloodshed in Sacramento and Santa Clara, and in Sonoma County skirmishes erupted on the Bodega and Sotoyome ranchos.

Stephen Smith, claimant of the Bodega Rancho, died in 1855; Tyler Curtis married his widow in 1856 and took over the rancho. Smith was easy-going about squatters, but the hard-nosed Curtis obtained a writ of eviction in 1859. The settlers refused to budge, arguing (wrongly) that their farms were not included in the grant boundary. Curtis went down to San Francisco and hired 50 bouncers

This Santa Rosa Saloon photo was taken at the turn of the century. The rear tables were for cards and light meals. Courtesy, Sonoma County Museum

to help in the eviction; his party landed at Petaluma wharf and marched toward Bodega. The squatters got wind of the invasion and 300 of them gathered with rifles to confront Curtis. Finding himself outnumbered, Curtis suddenly expressed a willingness to rent the land at bargain prices. The settlers then marched Curtis' army back to the Petaluma docks, ending the bloodless "Bodega War."

The Sotoyome affair ended less happily. Josephine Bailhache, daughter of Henry Fitch, proved her title to the Sotoyome Rancho around Healdsburg in 1858 and spent several years hassling with entrenched squatters. Local sentiment for squatters ran high, so in 1862 Sheriff J.M. Bowles sent all the way to Petaluma for militia to evict Alexander Skaggs and other settlers. A few months later Bailhache's workman Robert Ferguson was fatally shot while dismantling squatter fences. A.L. Norton, Bailhache's attorney and agent, retaliated by burning out Sotoyome squatters. "Some of the houses were good two-story buildings," Norton later wrote, "but I treated them as I would have done a lot of rats' nests . . . The squatters continued to hang around like the French soldiers around a burning Moscow until the elements drove them away to the hills, where some of them put up temporary adobes on the adjacent government land."

The scrappy Norton, a veteran of skirmishes over gold rush claims, made a profession out of evicting squatters from ranchos. He left the goldfields for a law practice in Placerville. When Placerville was gutted by fire in 1856, Norton moved down to Healdsburg and soon became the terror of local squatters.

The consistent losers in the land wars were the Indians, who were dispossessed of their native lands. A majority had already died from smallpox, cholera, and measles brought by whites. In 1837 a Mexican corporal from Sonoma contracted smallpox at Fort Ross and the disease spread inland. Whole villages in the Sonoma, Napa, and Suisin areas were wiped out. Julio Carrillo later told of seeing the bones of hundreds of Indian victims of the disease. Survivors watched settlers turn their ancestral lands into farms. Some found seasonal work in the fields. *Harper's Magazine* in 1861 chronicled the maltreatment of California Indians, reporting, "Of those that failed to perish from hunger or exposure, some were killed on the general prin-

ciple that they must have subsisted by stealing cattle." In 1853 the federal government set aside small reservations, but the *Petaluma Journal* of April 15, 1857, reported whites had killed 300 Indians near the Round Valley reservaton in Mendocino, in retaliation for Indians eating their cattle. Starvation, disease, murder, and kidnapping further reduced the numbers of native Americans, although isolated groups like the Kashaya Pomo near Stewart's Point maintained their traditions.

On May 25, 1861, the Pony Express brought the

OPPOSITE: These Santa Rosa High School ninth grade students posed for this photo in 1892. Courtesy, Sonoma County Museum

BELOW: As more families settled in Sonoma County, the need to educate and develop the children grew. Schools became the focal point in rural communities, and teachers were highly respected members of the community. Pictured here is the Kenwood School in the 1890s. Courtesy, Don Silverek Photography

news of the Confederate attack on Fort Sumter. The *Petaluma Journal* rushed out a special 8 p.m. edition on the start of the Civil War. California had entered the Union only 10 years previously as a free state, but Southern sympathy ran high in pockets, especially in Sonoma County, which had a high percentage of settlers with Confederate ties. In 1850 approximately one-quarter of Sonoma County's 562 residents (not counting Indians) were born in Missouri, Kentucky, Tennessee, or Virginia. An exception was Petaluma, initially settled by Yankee traders and foreign merchants. Californians were subject to Federal draft, but eastern Yankees didn't call upon their west coast brethren to fight, chiefly because of the cost of shuttling troops 3,000 miles to the battlefield. Relegated to the status of onlookers, Sonoma County partisans drew their own Mason-Dixon Line somewhere between Petaluma and Santa Rosa and waged war in the pages of rival newspapers.

Chief combatants were Samuel Cassiday, editor of the *Petaluma Argus,* and Thomas L. Thompson, editor of Santa Rosa's *Democrat.* Cassiday, raised in Ohio, tried his hand at dairy farming, mining, and teaching before turning to journalism as a supporter of Lincoln's Republican party and critic of the Southern "Copperheads." Thompson was a Virginian who started his newspaper career at age 12 in the office of the *West Virginian* before coming west. He started the *Petlauma Journal* at age 17, selling it in 1856 and buying Santa Rosa's *Sonoma Democrat* in 1860. Friends described him as "a man of great information, genial in his manners," but the words flung across the county between the *Democrat* and the *Argus* were anything but genial.

The *Democrat* blasted Lincoln's "unwise, unholy and fratricidal war," and railed against the anti-slavery movement and the "pretended amelioration of the African race" (September 4, 1862).

Lincoln's Emancipation Proclamation freeing the slaves had Thompson frothing, "By a mere stroke of the pen wielded in the hand of his Highness, Abraham Lincoln, three millions of Negro slaves, the property of the citizens of the United States, were declared forever free . . ." (January 3, 1863).

Cassiday charged that someone at the *Democrat,*

ABOVE: *An early REO truck loaded with sacks of hops at the Wood Ranch in Fulton portrays the fruitful harvest that hard work and rich Sonoma County soil could yield. Courtesy, Sonoma County Museum*

OPPOSITE: *Wild oats and hay covered the hills and valleys of this fertile countryside long before the first settlers moved into the area. Early work crews would move throughout the countryside, cutting and baling hay for the local settlers or for shipping. They would set up camp and work from dawn to dusk until they finished. Courtesy, Don Silverek Photography*

"malignant in his hatred to our Government, has taken possession of its columns" (April 7, 1864). The following week Thompson blasted the *Argus'* use of "low personalities and epithets which are the usual weapons of fools."

In Petaluma, the skirmish over the bell in the Petaluma Baptist Church was a microcosm of the Civil War. Manville "Matt" Doyle rescued the bell from a San Francisco junkyard in 1856, and it served as a town bell, tolling for emergencies as well as Sunday service. During the war, pro-Lincoln parishioners rang the bell for Union victories too, until churchgoers didn't know whether to put on their Sunday clothes, run out to fight a fire, or cheer for the Union. Doyle, a Southern sympathizer, was especially incensed since he helped buy the bell in the first place. Finally Doyle and friends came out with a block and tackle and liberated the bell, hiding it under potato sacks in a riverside warehouse. Then they nailed up the church for good measure. The next day Union Baptists rescued the bell and carted it back to church on a wagon draped with the American flag. They hoisted it back into the steeple and rang it loud and long, celebrating their victory but also cracking the bell. (Others say the bell cracked when it rang out the news of Lincoln's assassination. The bell, crack and all, is now on display at the Pioneer

Museum in San Francisco.)

Editorial warfare reached new lows after the 1864 election, when Lincoln took every California county except Sonoma. "Sonoma County has to stand as the Judas among the Brethren, as the black spot, and only spot on the coast where Treason has polled a large majority of votes," Cassiday wrote. He was gratified that Petaluma and Bloomfield went for Lincoln. "But there are other precincts where the people are of the lowest type of the Gorilla tribe, wild and uncultivated savages, from the wilds of Arkansas, Missouri, Texas, etc., who can neither read nor write, nor think" (November 11, 1864). Thompson countered, ". . . we of Sonoma county have the happy reflection that those who may live in after years to regret the triumph of despotism in free America, cannot say that we did it."

The South capitulated in the spring of 1865, and the venomous exchanges subsided. When John Wilkes Booth assassinated Lincoln on April 14, 1865, Thompson issued an edition, heavily lined in black, out of respect—and fear. San Franciscans, outraged at the president's murder, sacked the offices of five Secessionist papers in the city. In Petaluma, the boys of Hueston's Guard saddled up with vague intentions of riding north and doing the same to the *Democrat*. Local lore says the marauders rode as far north as the Washoe House tavern, where the excellent beer distracted them and put an end to the invasion of Santa Rosa.

With the war over, Petalumans, Santa Rosans, and their neighbors returned to their customary preoccupations: raising cows, chickens, grapes, hops, and apples—and getting them all to market. The area was on the threshold of tremendous expansion. The coming of the railroad would transform Sonoma County from a quiet rural enclave into a major supplier of produce to the world.

Cycling became a popular sport in Sonoma County soon after the Civil War, when the velocipede, or three-wheeler, was the favored cycle. By the 1890s the two-wheeler with a large front wheel became the cycle of choice. The Empire Wheelmen, organized in 1880, promoted cycling with ambitious trips such as a two-week jaunt to Yosemite and back. The Wheelmen leased a clubhouse that still stands on Cherry Street in Santa Rosa, and met for noon lunches, cards, and billiards. Courtesy, Sonoma County Museum

CHAPTER FOUR

Commerce in Motion

Railroads came to Sonoma County in the 1870s. Steam locomotives quickened the pulse of commerce and boosted trade with the Port of San Francisco, providing worldwide markets for timber, eggs, grapes, hops, and produce. Nothing in Sonoma County's history changed the area so fast as the railroads. Maritime transport was crucial, too. Schooners cruised the North Coast to pick up timber; steamboats on the estuaries provided the vital link between San Francisco and rail lines that ended at Petaluma, Sausalito, and San Rafael.

In the two decades before the advent of rail lines, however, stages and ox-carts hauled passengers and freight. In summer, stagecoach passengers covered their faces with bandanas to keep out clouds of dust. In the winter drivers coaxed their teams along highways that turned into rivers of mud. The driver's job was prestigious but rugged; passengers had a rough time of it, too. The stage from Santa Rosa, for instance, was traveling downhill toward Petaluma one rainy spring day in 1864 when the coach hit a stump and threw the driver from his seat. "The horses ran a short distance and turned into a narrow by-lane, where they soon fetched up against a fence," the *Petaluma Argus* reported. "The passengers . . . did not stand on the order of their going, but emptied themselves out of the stage in a hurry." A blinding rain was blamed for the mishap.

Stages pulled by teams of six horses made daily trips up the central highway that ran north from Petaluma through Santa Rosa, Windsor, Healdsburg, Geyserville, and Cloverdale. Another major thoroughfare went from Petaluma through Bloomfield, Valley Ford, Bodega Corners, Bodega Bay, and on up the coast through Fort Ross to Gualala. One of the county's oldest roads went from Petaluma to Sonoma and up the valley through Glen Ellen to Santa Rosa. Another began at Petaluma and went north through Sebastopol to Green Valley.

Where stages run there will naturally be stage robbers—or "footpads," as unmounted robbers were called. Determined bandits strung a rope across the road near Green Valley and halted the Miller and Co. stage from Santa Rosa to Bodega in December 1871, escaping with $286 from the Wells Fargo box.

Wells Fargo's nemesis was Black Bart, a notoriously genteel bandit who plagued the company up and down the state between 1875 and 1883. The lone bandit pulled 28 robberies—several in Sonoma and Mendocino counties—always with the same modus operandi. A lone man on foot disguised by a flour sack mask appeared on the road, pointed his double-barrel shotgun at the driver, and demanded the Wells Fargo box and U.S. mail. After his fourth robbery—the first in Sonoma County—the previously unnamed robber left behind an empty cash box, a poem, and his nickname.

Coast rancher George W. Call was riding south to catch the Duncans Mills train to San Francisco on August 3, 1877, when he came upon a man drinking from a stream three miles below Fort Ross. The fellow jumped up and asked if the stage had gone by. Call said the stage would be along soon and continued on his way. The man hurried on to Shotgun Point, robbed the stage, and left a tantalizing note in the otherwise empty express box: "I've labored long and hard for bread, for honor and for riches, but on my corns too long you've tred, you fine-haired sons of bitches." The verse was signed "Black Bart, the PO8."

The persistent bandit robbed the same stage in 1880 and held up the Cloverdale stage in 1882 and 1883. Bart's luck ran out in 1883 when he left behind a handkerchief during a botched holdup. Wells Fargo detective J.B. Hume traced the kerchief's laundry mark to a San Francisco laundry and arrested C.E. Boles, alias Charles Bolton, who was posing as a distinguished, middle-aged mining engineer. Boles was released after four years in San Quentin and promised to go straight. The warden asked if he planned to write any more poetry. Boles replied, "I've just told you, warden, I promise to commit no more crimes." Then he vanished. Rumors persisted that Wells Fargo paid him a stipend to refrain from robbing their stages.

The most celebrated stage rides went to the Geysers in the hills northeast of Healdsburg. William Elliott, tracking a bear, was the first white settler to come upon the geothermal fields; they soon became a renowned tourist spectacle as famous in their day as Yosemite is now. Historian J.P. Munro-Fraser wrote in 1880, "Of all the noted places in Sonoma county, indeed on the Pacific coast, the most famous is the Geysers . . . It is positively a most 'uncanny' place." All the county's major hotels advertised stage trips to the Geysers. Roads were built from Healds-

ABOVE: The stagecoach, a buckboard, and some locals paused for this captured 1875 moment in front of the John Folks Hotel. Courtesy, Sonoma County Library

OPPOSITE, TOP: Giant trees like this one were felled throughout the Redwood Empire during the early days of the lumber industry. Courtesy, Don Silverek Photography

OPPOSITE, BOTTOM: Vast redwood forests attracted lumbermen to the county as the demand for construction materials rose with the population. This 1880s shot, taken in the redwoods at Guerneville on the Russian River, seems to indicate a gathering of labor and management, or perhaps a group of sightseers posing in front of the felled redwood trunk. Courtesy, Sonoma County Museum

burg and Cloverdale, and Colonel A.G. Godwin put up the two-story Geysers Hotel with a veranda overlooking sulphurous Pluton Canyon. Journalist Bayard Taylor, whose writings publicized the Geysers, visited in 1862. "The rocks burn under you," he wrote. "You are enveloped in fierce heat, strangled by puffs of diabolical vapor, and stunned by the awful, hissing, spitting, sputtering, roaring, threatening sounds—as if a dozen steamboats blowing through their escape-pipes, had aroused the ire of ten-

thousand hell-cats."

No less famous was the hair-raising ride to the Geysers, especially in the hands of driver Clark Foss, who made a handy living escorting parties there. Foss was legendary for his bravado and casual disregard of precipices as he raced along. The heart-stopping trip over the hills was the stagecoach version of a roller coaster ride. Robert Louis Stevenson, commenting on Foss' cult standing, wrote, "Along the unfenced, abominable mountain roads, he launches his team with small regard to human life or the doctrine of probabilities. Flinching travellers, who behold themselves coasting eternity at every corner, look with natural admiration at their driver's huge, impassive, fleshy countenance."

Ships provided the only reliable transport for isolated communities along the rocky Sonoma coast. Commerce increased dramatically in the 1850s when the demand for lumber rose and mills sprang up to meet it. A handful of Northern California ports—Mendocino, Noyo, Humboldt, and Crescent City—could accommodate large boats. The rest had anchorage only for "dog-hole" schooners, so-called because they could weigh anchor in a spot just big enough for a dog to turn around in. Every little cove along the Sonoma coast was a dog-hole port where schooners called regularly for timber, split wood, and tanbark oak used in the tanning process. Schooners with crews of half a dozen would stay offshore, loading and unloading goods with a sliding chute that hung out over the water. Railroad ties, cordwood, and even passengers would come flying down the chute while a deck hand caught them at the

other end. The major commodity was lumber from mills at Fort Ross, Salt Point, Helmke's Mill, Fisk's Landing, and mills on the Gualala River. In the 1870s the largest mill on the Sonoma coast was Duncans Mill, producing 25,000 feet of lumber per day. The Duncan brothers, Samuel and Alexander, had a mill at Salt Point; they relocated near the mouth of the Russian River and in the late 1870s moved again farther upstream (to present-day Duncans Mills)

near the new railroad.

Redwood was a favorite material for construction. Douglas fir, available on the coast in great quantities, was among the finest materials for ship building. From the 1850s to the 1920s, the West Coast was the world center of wooden ship building.

The jagged coastline with its hidden reefs and sudden winter storms claimed more than its share of ships.

ABOVE: Petaluma's prosperity was due chiefly to its river commerce. The Steamer Gold Line, with a connection to the Petaluma and Santa Rosa Railroad, operated the Gold, which carried passengers, and the Petaluma, a freight boat. They churned back and forth between Petaluma and the San Francisco waterfront. Pictured here is the passenger steamer Gold. Courtesy, Don Silverek Photography

OPPOSITE: The dairy industry was another prominent enterprise in Petaluma. This dairy farm was photographed sometime around 1880. Courtesy, Don Silverek Photography

RIGHT: Bodega Creamery seems to be experiencing an early morning rush to pick up fresh cream for delivery. Bodega Creamery sits in the heart of the dairyland in Sonoma County. Some areas such as this have changed very little throughout the years. Cattle can still be seen grazing on the coastal hills and houses and buildings have remained intact and well maintained. Courtesy, Sonoma County Museum

The *Abraham Lincoln,* owned by rancher A. Richardson of Stewart's Point, was carrying 75,000 feet of lumber when it was battered against the cliffs at Stewart's Point in 1875. Two vessels were wrecked on the same night in 1854 at the Fish Rocks just north of Gualala; one was the steamer *Arispa,* which hit the reef in rough seas. The captain drained his cargo of liquor and jerryrigged a life raft out of empty barrels. One passenger reported "he never saw as many woe-begone visages on one occasion as there were on the deck of the Arispa when the sparkling liquor gurgled from the bung-holes and passed out through the scuppers into the ocean."

One of the later wrecks was the *Pomona,* steaming

north toward Eureka on St. Patrick's Day in 1908 when it struck a sunken reef two miles south of Fort Ross. The Call family, coming down from their Fort Ross ranch, helped the 84 passengers get safely to shore.

In southern Sonoma County, estuaries linking Sonoma and Petaluma to San Pablo Bay were ready-made avenues for commerce. Boats on these tidal creeks provided a regular and cheap mode of transport to San Francisco. Traffic on the Petaluma estuary began in earnest in the 1850s when Charles Minturn, the bay's "Ferryboat King," instituted service to Lakeview six miles downstream from Petaluma. Packet boats and schooners skimmed over mudflats all the way to Petaluma, and eventually the creek was dredged so the biggger steamers could get through. Stage lines and later the Petaluma and Santa Rosa Railroad funneled people and freight to the Petaluma docks for passage to San Francisco. River commerce was a major factor in the town's prosperity. Steamers, scow schooners, and barges carried wool, butter, cream, eggs, live chicks, and incubators down the twisting tidal river to the bay. By the turn of the century the Petaluma River was the third busiest waterway in the state, after the Sacramento and the San Joaquin.

Steamers, introduced to California during the gold rush, went down the San Joaquin or all the way up the Sacramento River to Red Bluff. The Steamer Gold Line, with a connection to the Petaluma and Santa Rosa Railroad, operated the *Gold,* which carried passengers, and the *Petaluma,* a freight

boat that churned back and forth between Petaluma and the San Francisco waterfront. *Petaluma #1* was built in 1857 and was destroyed in 1900. *Petaluma #2* caught fire at the Petaluma wharf in 1914 and burned to the waterline with a full cargo; the crew had to push the boat out into the river to save the wharf. Its engines were saved and installed in its successor, *Petaluma #3*.

The first *Gold* was just as unlucky. It was fully loaded and tied up at the Petaluma docks when a midnight fire broke out onboard. A strong wind pinned it against the dock, so that boat, wharf, and warehouse all went up in flames.

Petaluma #3 had a round bow and a scow-like bottom. It was a plain, work-horse boat, designed expressly for the Petaluma poultry trade with its engine room and stack in the rear so the heat wouldn't damage the perishable eggs in the bow.

Eventually the irrigation required for immense farms depleted the rivers, and the steamboat network shrank. Tugboats pulling barges took over river freight.

The Petaluma run was the last survivor of stern-wheeler ferryboat commerce in California. After he docked for the last time in Petaluma, Skipper Jack Urton, who had a flair for the historic moment, made a final entry in his log for August 24, 1950: "Arr. Petaluma 10:45 p.m. . . . After 35 year, 8 mo. and 10 days, we tie up for good. This ends 103 years of sternwheel river navigation on SF bay and tributaries.—John H. Urton, Master."

It was the railroad that really opened up the vast agricultural and timber regions to steady and lucrative trade. The narrow gauge through Marin and western Sonoma County carried vast amounts of timber to San Francisco markets. The Petaluma and Santa Rosa Electric Railway carried milk and apples from Sebastopol's Gold Ridge district to the Petaluma docks. Broad gauge lines in the Sonoma and Santa Rosa valleys gave Sonoma County farmers access to eastern markets, especially after refrigerated railroad cars were introduced to preserve perishable fruits,

OPPOSITE, TOP: With the arrival of the railroad, production in the lumber industry increased dramatically. By 1886 a spur ran seven miles along Austin Creek to Cazadero, making accessible vast tracts of timberland owned by some of the railroad directors. Redwood was the primary freight. Courtesy, Don Silverek Photography

OPPOSITE, BOTTOM: George Guerne and Thomas Heald owned this large lumber mill in an area called Big Bottom (now known as Guerneville). In the 1870s the largest mill on the Sonoma coast was Duncans Mill, producing 25,000 feet of lumber per day. Courtesy, Don Silverek Photography

BELOW: Railroads came to Sonoma County in the 1870s, quickening the pulse of commerce and boosting trade with the Port of San Francisco. Courtesy, Don Silverek Photography

vegetables, and dairy products.

The first railroad enterprise was a modest one, however. In 1862, Minturn, the mogul of ferry traffic, improved his shipping system by laying three miles of track between Haystack Landing and Petaluma. The Petaluma and Haystack Railroad was the third railroad in the state.

Petalumans considered Minturn to be frugal to a fault, an opinion that was explosively confirmed when the train was about to leave Petaluma station on August 27, 1866. Minturn's regular engineer had quit, and substitute engineer Joe Levitt was in the cab firing up the Atlas locomotive. Minturn saved a few bucks by having Levitt act as fireman as well as engineer, but Levitt was apparently unaware it was his job to maintain the water level in the boiler. The boiler was bone dry, and when the steam gauge hit 120 pounds, the boiler blew. Pistons and chunks of locomotive flew in all directions. John McNear, one of Petaluma's leading citizens, had just bent over to tie his shoelace when a hunk of twisted metal whizzed over his head. The blast killed six men, including Levitt. Fortunately most passengers had left the platform and boarded the train, which shielded them from the cataclysm. Minturn never made good on his promise to replace the locomotive; for the rest of its 11-year history a team of horses pulled the P & H up and down the tracks.

As the 1860s drew to a close, Sonoma County had roughly 19,000 inhabitants, and most of them saw a railroad as their ticket to greater prosperity. Two routes had their partisans. Banker John Frisbie, General Vallejo's son-in-law, proposed a rail line from Vallejo to Cloverdale by way of Sonoma and Santa Rosa, a route that would freeze out Petaluma, the county's biggest town. Petalumans, naturally, favored a Petaluma-to-Cloverdale route. Sonoma County supervisors offered a subsidy of $5,000 per mile to the first company laying 10 miles of track.

One of the men to take up the challenge was Peter Donahue, an enterprising native of Glasgow, Scotland, who became a captain of industry after migrating in his late 20s to California during the gold rush. Starting as an ordinary machinist,

he created San Francisco's Union Iron Works, a prosperous factory that built mining equipment and locomotives. Then Donahue turned his boundless energy to railroading itself. Donahue purchased the San Francisco and North Pacific Railroad and built a line north from Petaluma toward Santa Rosa. Regular service on the line started in October 1870. On the last day of 1870 Donahue invited San Francisco bigwigs to an inaugural ride from Petaluma all the way to Santa Rosa.

Donahue continued to lay track north of Santa Rosa, but early in 1871 met his match. Frisbie had contributed $100,000 to the California Pacific Railroad to see a rail line built north via Sonoma Valley. Technically, the supervisors had committed themselves to a $5,000-a-mile subsidy to the first railroad laying a line all the way through the county. Soon the SF&NP and the Cal P were in a race toward Healdsburg along parallel tracks, Donahue's Irish workers digging madly on one side and Cal P's Chinese coolies swinging picks on the other. The

marathon came to an abrupt halt when Donahue sold out to Cal P for $750,000. Two years later he bought it back for a cool million. By then the rails ran all the way to Cloverdale.

The SF&NP line brought prosperity to Santa Rosa, Healdsburg, and the towns in central Sonoma County, but was too far east for the timbermen of the lower Russian River. George Guerne and Thomas Heald owned the

largest mill in an area called Big Bottom, later called
Stumptown (for obvious reasons), and finally known as
Guerneville. Frank, Antoine, and Joseph Korbel had originally gone into the lumber business to build boxes for
their San Francisco cigar business and wound up as timbermen. Together they went to Donahue, offering free
wood for trestles if he would build a line to the heart of
redwood country. Donahue built the Fulton and
Guerneville Railroad in 1876, connecting to the SF&NP at
Fulton.

A separate narrow-gauge line, linking communities
in the western parts of Sonoma and Marin counties, began
at the ferry terminal in Sausalito. Owners of the North
Pacific Coast Railroad (later the North Shore and then
Northwestern Pacific) felt the less expensive slim gauge
could penetrate the region's dense forests and narrow
canyons. By 1873 1,300 Chinese laborers were out with
picks and shovels preparing the line while other workers
built trestles over countless gulches. The Brown's Canyon
trestle south of Howards was then the highest in the United States, and there were 68 other trestles between Point
Reyes and Monte Rio. Freestone was the terminus for a
couple of years while the workers graded the line up to the
575-foot summit at Howards (later Occidental), named
after "Dutch Bill" Howard, one of the earliest settlers.

With the influx of railroad crews, Valley Ford and
Freestone enjoyed a brief boomtown prosperity. Rancher
Hollis Hinds built a 32-room hotel near the Freestone
depot, and other hotels and rooming houses flourished.
In Septebmer 1876 the railroad reached the Russian River
at Monte Rio. Not everyone was
glad the line was finished.
Watchman T. Perry was on night
duty in May 1877 when he spotted a trestle on fire near Freestone. Perry's nine-year-old boy
roused a crowd who put the fire
out before it consumed the
bridge. The arsonist torched
another trestle in August but this
time section boss M. Shea caught
the perpetrator red-handed. The
culprit was Hinds, who hoped to
save his hotel by drumming up
some business from workmen
who would stay in his hotel while
they rebuilt the trestles.

Narrow-gauge locomotives

ABOVE: After tracks were laid in the 1870s, Bay Area residents could hop on ferries that connected to rail lines to Sonoma Valley or the Russian River. Here, tourists prepare to board the train at Monte Rio. Courtesy, Don Silverek Photography

LEFT: Resorts flourished along the tracks at Mirabel, Hilton, Rio Nido, Guerneville, Camp Meeker, Occidental, and Monte Rio, where this railroad trestle is located. Accommodations on the Russian River ranged from floored tents to multi-story hotels nestled among the redwoods. Sully's Resort in Monte Rio sent its autobus to the Monte Rio train station to collect guests. Courtesy, Don Silverek Photography

OPPOSITE: Bull teams were used to haul heavy timber in the early days of the lumber industry. This timber site near Occidental appears to have been stripped of its stand of timber. Courtesy, Sonoma County Museum

warmed up at the ferry building in Sausalito and chugged northwest toward Point Reyes, picking up clams and oysters from Marshall and Bivalve on the edge of Tomales Bay. At Tomales they picked up hay and milk before steaming through a tunnel and stopping at Valley Ford and Bodega for potatoes and hogs. North of Freestone the track entered timber country, cresting at Howards and then descending to the Russian River at Monte Rio. Steaming uphill, the locomotive made periodic stops to take on water; crew and passengers would hop off the train and toss some cordwood on board to replenish fuel for the engine.

Small mills had been turning out lumber for local use for years, but with the arrival of the railroad, production went into high gear. Mills like Streeten's and Tyrone flourished along the narrow-gauge line. In 1876 Alexander Duncan moved his mill several miles upstream to be near the railroad, settling at the present site of Duncans Mills.

By 1886 a spur ran 7.4 miles along Austin Creek to Cazadero, chiefly to take advantage of vast tracts of timber owned by some of the railroads' directors. Redwood, an ideal wood for buildings, was the primary freight. Tanbark oak, a wood that contained more tannin than any other tree, was another prized cargo. Chinese woodcutters and, later, newly arrived Italian immigrants would peel the tannin-bearing bark off in the spring when the sap was running, then cut the rest up for cordwood. Tanbark oak was an important Sonoma County product until the 1930s when a synthetic compound for tanning leather was developed in Germany.

The county-wide railroad network was a tremendous boon to farmers and businessmen. By the end of the century, Sonoma County was one of the most prosperous counties in the nation, the produce from its ranches and farms speeding to markets undreamed of in the mid-1800s.

Every summer adults and children practically lived in the fields, working all day to glean the thumb-sized hops from 15- to 20-foot vines. These families of hops pickers lived near the Russian River area in the late nineteenth century. Courtesy, Sonoma County Museum

Immigrants and Agriculture

With railroads to speed Sonoma County goods to market, several products came into their own. Sonoma County folks had harvested timber, apples, eggs, and dairy products for themselves, but suddenly these goods became big business with this quantum leap in transportation. And with the innovation of ice cars, Sonoma County produce could be rushed fresh to eastern markets. Agriculture flourished to such an extent that in the 1920 census Sonoma County was listed as the eighth most productive county in the United States. In 1937 it was still in 10th place.

Immigrants played key roles in the burgeoning industries. As the fabled land of opportunity, America lured adventurous souls from all the countries of the world, and Sonoma County drew more than its share. Italians, Swiss, Irish, British, Germans, Portuguese, and Chinese all played their part in nineteenth-century Sonoma County, just as other nationalities—Japanese, Mexicans, Ethiopians, Cambodians—would in the twentieth century.

No other immigrant group was so tied to the history of the railroads as the Chinese. Although some railroad tycoons like Peter Donahue refused to hire Orientals, a flood of Chinese came to California during the 1860s and 1870s. Hundreds of Chinese "coolies" worked on the narrow gauge through western Marin and Sonoma and stayed to work in timber, farming, or household jobs like cooking. By 1880, 125 Chinese had congregated to form a Santa Rosa Chinatown, and many more worked in rural areas.

While times were good the white population of California lived in uneasy coexistence with the Orientals. But the 1870s brought a widespread economic downturn that prompted whites to blame the Chinese for their economic woes. By 1886, disgruntled white workers clamored for the expulsion of California's quarter-million Chinese.

Prejudice found its way into the editorials of California's newspapers. "Go where you may in the state you find swarms of these people," editorialized the *Sonoma Democrat* in December 1885. "They are in every hotel, in nearly all private houses where servants are employed, in the laundries, in shops and stores, in the mines, on the farm—in fact everywhere. The population of the state is about one million, one-fourth of whom are Chinamen. Now it is evident that Chinese immigration must be stopped or the ruin of California is inevitable." Chinese were barred from becoming citizens and voters, and Governor George Stoneman stood firmly behind his white constituents, declaring that "the Chinese . . . are crowding the Caucasian race out of many avenues of employment."

Anti-Chinese associations and anti-coolie leagues sprang up all over California. Their common weapon was boycott. Santa Rosans met at the skating rink in January 1886, pledging to "rid themselves of the Chinese evil." The Healdsburg Anti-Coolie Club secured the signatures of 700 locals who vowed to withhold money from Chinese laborers and merchants.

Prejudice against Chinese in Sonoma County was further inflamed by a sensational murder near Cloverdale in January 1886. Jesse Wickersham and his wife were found shotgunned in their farmhouse, and their missing cook, Ah Tai, was blamed for the murder. Ah Tai vanished on a steamer leaving San Francisco, but he and, by association, his countrymen were tried in the papers. "The sentiment against the Chinese runs high in consequence of this act of heathen brutality, and the Chinese during yesterday kept in close quarters," reported the *Sonoma Democrat* on January 30, 1886. "Chinese cooks will find great difficulty in securing employment in this section of the country hereafter." In the wake of the murder, crowds turned out at mass meetings—2,000 in Petaluma and 1,000 in Cloverdale—to press for a universal boycott of Chinese businesses.

Prejudice had become a matter of law in 1882 when the federal government, bowing to pressure from California, ratified a new treaty with China that prohibited immigration of Chinese for 10 years. The ban was renewed in 1892 and 1902. Despite the widespread boycott of the 1880s, some early immigrants stayed on and found employment with sympathetic neighbors.

Like so many others, Italians came to California during the gold rush, and by 1851 there were about 600 Italians in San Francisco. Some rushed to Placer country, while others like Domenico Ghirardelli made a fortune in mercantile trades. In 1880 the cost of passage from Italy to New York dropped to $40; large numbers of Northern Italians migrated from Genoa and Turin and

ABOVE: Vineyard workers pick grapes for the Simi Brothers Winery in Healds-burg around 1900. Courtesy, Don Silverek Photography

OPPOSITE, TOP: Genoese banker Andrea Sbarbaro founded the Italian-Swiss Agricultural Colony at Asti in 1881. With chemist Pietro Rossi as his head winemaker, the colony began to prosper after a few lean years. Production was so abundant in 1897 that a 500,000-gallon capacity rock reservoir was built to store the wine. It is no wonder that workers received, in addition to wages, all the wine they could drink. Courtesy, Sonoma County Museum

OPPOSITE, BOTTOM: The grape harvest was a family affair throughout the 1800s and early 1900s. Here families harvest grapes in the Simi Vineyards at the turn of the century. Courtesy, Don Silverek Photography

the Lombard vineyard regions, bringing their expertise and passion for grape growing with them. Many by-passed the large eastern cities of the U.S. and headed straight for the slopes of California. The soil and climate of California are similar to that of Tuscany and other regions of Northern Italy. Farmers and vintners from the north of Italy found their pastoral life was readily trans-planted to the slopes and valleys of Sonoma County. Between 1890 and 1920 a large influx of Italians settled in the Russian River Valley between Healdsburg and

Cloverdale to create winemaking dynasties.

The man who gave many Italian farmers their start in Sonoma County was Andrea Sbarbaro, a Genoese banker who envisioned a semi-utopian community for unemployed farmers from Italy and Switzerland. With chemist Pietro Rossi as his head winemaker, Sbarbaro founded the Italian-Swiss Agricultural Colony at Asti in 1881. Workers received wages plus all the wine they could drink. After a few lean years, the colony prospered. The 1897 vintage was so great that there was not enough cooperage in all of California to contain it. To store excess wine, Italian-Swiss constructed a solid rock reservoir 80 feet by 34 feet by 25 feet deep—the largest wine tank in the world, holding 500,000 gallons. When the tank was emptied in the spring of 1898, 200 workers held a dance inside it with an orchestra seated in the center. By 1910 Italian-Swiss had the largest capacity of any winery in the U.S.—8.5 million gallons.

Italian wine dynasties—the Sebastianis, Simis, Marti-nis, and Pratis—were the rule. But Italians did not have a monopoly on Sonoma County grape growing. German immigrant Jacob Gundlach was among the early wine growers in the Sonoma Valley. Gundlach left Germany in 1850 for California, but his plans did not include mining. He planted 400 acres of vineyards, constructed a stone winery on his Rhinefarm Estate near Sonoma, and in 1862 went into partnership with fellow Bavarian Charles Bundschu. Their wines gained a following, first in San Francisco, then on the East Coast, and by the turn of the century the Gundlach-Bundschu Wine Company warehouse in San Francisco covered an entire city block.

Pennsylvanian Isaac DeTurk came to Santa Rosa in 1862 and planted his first Yulupa Vineyard' in 1862. By the 1880s his three cellars at Bennett Valley, Santa Rosa, and Cloverdale were producing 250,000 gallons of wine and 10,000 gallons of brandy a year. DeTurk's wines won four first places at the 1881 state fair. During the 1880s and 1890s he served as state viticultural commissioner for the Sonoma district.

DeTurk was also a pioneer in enlightened labor rela-

tions, criticizing other growers for their casual attitude toward field hands. "I think these proprietors are to blame for crowding the laborers into their barns like horses and cattle and allowing them to sleep out in their haystacks in the fields during harvest time," DeTurk wrote. "I have built a nice tenement house for my men and give them good food and a good table to eat at, and I find my men more willing to stop with me."

The three Korbel brothers, Francis, Anton, and Joseph, came to California from Czechoslovakia. Originally machinists and locksmiths, they turned to the cigar business and in the 1860s bought 6,000 acres of timber east of Guerneville to log wood for cigar boxes. Later they switched from timber to grapes, using the land they cleared along the Russian River. To satisfy the champagne taste of high-flying San Francisco society, the Korbels imported a champagne master from their homeland and became U.S. pioneers of the *méthode champenoise*—a style of making

ABOVE: Many families in Sonoma County had only grapevines and a wine cellar to their name. This photo shows the Baldini family making wine in the basement of their home in Santa Rosa. Courtesy, Don Silverek Photography

TOP: Francis, Anton, and Joseph Korbel came to California from Czechoslovakia. Originally machinists and locksmiths, they turned to the cigar business and in the 1860s bought 6,000 acres of timberland east of Guerneville to log wood for cigar boxes. This photo depicts the Korbel sawmill, four miles north of Guerneville. The Korbels would later make their name in the wine industry. Courtesy, Don Silverek Photography

The Korbel Brothers diversified, and the prune industry was one of many activities at the site of their winery. Here prunes dry at the winery near Guerneville. Courtesy, Don Silverek Photography

ABOVE: For decades, hops—an essential ingredient in beer—was a big crop in the area. Acres of rich floodland along the county's creeks were the prime areas for hop ranches. After the 1870s ranches sprang up along the Laguna de Santa Rosa and Santa Rosa Creek, as well as up and down the Russian River. Today Sonoma County's hop kilns are falling into ruin, although some have been transformed into picturesque settings for wineries. Courtesy, William Beedie Photo Collection

OPPOSITE, TOP: Prussian immigrant William Metzger started the Santa Rosa Steam Brewery in 1872, supplying saloons that sold beer for a nickel a glass. Frank and Joseph Grace bought Metzger out in 1897 to begin the Grace Brothers Brewing Company. Here, a group of Grace Brothers employees enjoy their product in front of the brewery. Courtesy, Don Silverek Photography

OPPOSITE, BOTTOM: Youngsters who picked hops for extra money were generally paid one cent per pound, and were able to pick perhaps 100 pounds of hops per day. Courtesy, Sonoma County Museum

champagne directly in the bottle.

The wine industry continued to prosper. Agostin Haraszthy had shrewdly imported the pick of European vines in the 1860s. By the turn of the century Sonoma County was known through the country as a premier wine region. In 1875 the county produced almost 3.4 million gallons of wine, more than any county in California, a full 41 percent of the state's total wine production. (Napa County was fourth with a meager 873,000 gallons.) Wine grape tonnage for the county was 32,524 tons for 1890, and by 1910 it had more than doubled to 68,778. Before Prohibition, there were more than 200 wineries in the area and as many as 40,000 acres planted in vines.

The major setback to the industry was the phylloxera pest that also ravaged the vineyards of Europe. The pest, a louse that attacked the roots of the vines, did the greatest damage in the Sonoma Valley, showing up there around 1875. The infestation spread north and appeared in the

Russian River Valley by the 1890s. Growers tried flooding the vineyards or applying chemicals, but most eventually threw in the towel and dug up entire vineyards, replanting with resistant vines on which to graft their fine varieties. The grafting method worked; by the turn of the century Sonoma County vines were replanted and thriving.

Winemaking with its venerable old world traditions was perhaps the most prestigious Sonoma County enterprise, but other agricultural products came to prominence in the nineteenth century as well, among them hops, eggs, and apples.

Ranchers planted hops in the rich bottom land around the Russian River and the Laguna starting in the 1870s. Every August, men, women, and children moved out to the fields to glean hops from the 20-foot vines; the annual harvest took on the quality of a community festival, with families camping in the fields. Hop kilns, used for drying the crop, dotted the west county. (The best-preserved example is at Hop Kiln Winery, lovingly restored by owner Martin Griffin and listed on the National Register of Historic Places.) Hops put the bitter tang into beer, so breweries naturally sprang up not far from hop ranches. Prussian immigrant William Metzger started

With the hop ranches came beer, and basement bottling operations such as this one sprang up throughout the county. The Santa Rosa Steam Brewery, later known as Grace Brothers Brewing Company, began supplying beer to nearby saloons. Courtesy, Sonoma County Museum

the Santa Rosa Steam Brewery in 1872, supplying saloons that sold the suds for a nickel a glass. Frank and Joseph Grace bought Metzger out in 1897; Grace Brothers Brewing Company bottled beer under the Acme label, which became one of the state's favorite brands. Ranchers shipped hops in 200-pound bales to ports as far away as Australia.

Petaluma rose to prominence as the "Egg Capital of the World," largely through the efforts of two inventors

and an astute promoter. Canadian Lyman Byce came to Petaluma in 1878 and there perfected the modern incubator. The concept was centuries old, but Byce found a way to keep incubator temperatures steady. Byce's incubator went on display at the Sonoma-Marin Agricultural Society Fair in 1879, and it was a big hit at the 1883 state fair. The aisles of the exhibit pavilion were packed with curious onlookers who crowded around the incubator to watch chicks emerging from their shells. Ladies, caught between the warm incubators and the pressing crowds, fainted from the heat, and watchmen reported many visitors left the pavilion with cheeping sounds coming from their pockets.

Christopher Nisson, a native of Schleswig-Holstein on the German-Danish border, came to Petaluma in 1864 and raised brown leghorns in Two Rock. Using Byce's new incubator, he hatched chicks for his neighbors; by the 1880s Nisson had 2,000 laying hens and was the region's first commercial egg rancher. Nisson developed a better brooder using better ventilation, and he developed a balanced feed for poultry. His articles on chicken raising drew experts from all over Europe. In 1898 Nisson moved his equipment to the town of Petaluma and founded the Pioneer Hatchery, America's first commercial hatchery. With improved incubators and brooders, Petaluma became a leading poultry center as rival hatcheries were established.

It was not until 1918, however, that Petaluma consciously billed itself as the world's egg basket. At the close of World War I, Petaluma's Chamber of Commerce hired H.W. Kerrigan to survey the town's industrial potential. To their surprise, Kerrigan advised the town fathers to put all their eggs in one basket and promote the poultry business.

Petaluma, calculated Kerrigan, had more hatcheries and poultry breeding farms than anywhere else in the world. Under his direction the chamber spent $50,000 to publicize Petaluma as the "Egg Capital of the World." They invited national newsreel companies to film chicken and egg scenes and the town's Egg Day parades. Petaluma eggs were shipped worldwide.

Hundreds of ranchers came down with chicken fever and moved to the area to start their own ranches with a few hundred chickens each. Among them was a group of Jewish socialists who came to Petaluma to establish a rural community, seeing agricultural life as a haven for refugees from the sweatshops of eastern cities. The first Jewish families came to Petaluma before 1915; the next year they helped organize a Poultry Producers cooperative that also served as a savings bank. By 1925 there were 100 Jewish

ABOVE: In 1918 Petaluma consciously started billing itself as the world's egg basket. At the close of World War I, the Petaluma Chamber of Commerce hired H.W. Kerrigan to survey the town's industrial potential and suggest a new direction. Kerrigan discovered that Petaluma had more hatcheries and poultry breeding farms than anywhere else in the world. Courtesy, Don Silverek Photography

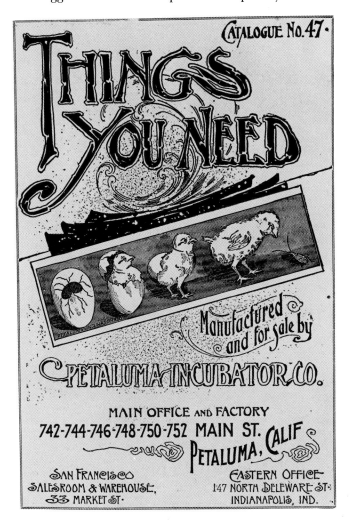

LEFT: Catalog shopping was the primary method of obtaining "Things you need" in the late 1800s and early 1900s. This ad from Catalogue No. 47 marketed the improved incubators that were responsible for establishing Petaluma as a leading poultry center. By 1904 the Petaluma Hatchery had a capacity for hatching 500,000 eggs at once. Courtesy, Sonoma County Museum

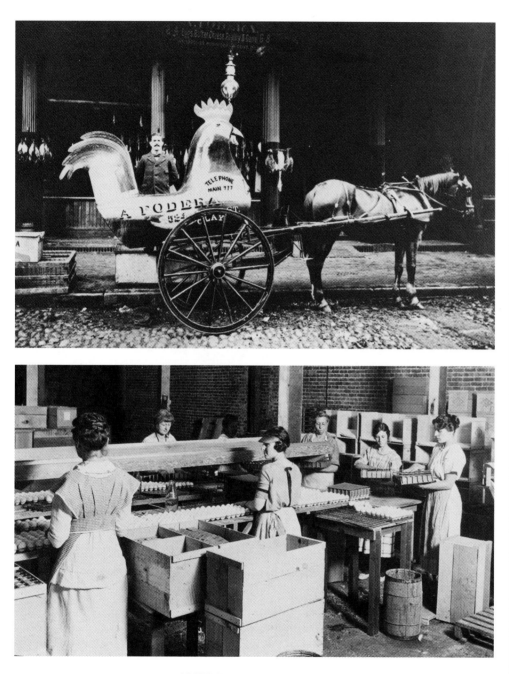

ABOVE: Women work at an egg packing plant in Petaluma in the early 1900s. Courtesy, Don Silverek Photography

TOP: Under the direction of H.W. Kerrigan, the Petaluma Chamber of Commerce spent $50,000 to publicize Petaluma as the "Egg Capital of World." National newsreel companies filmed hatcheries and the town's Egg Day parades. This horse-drawn chicken was photographed in about 1920. Courtesy, Don Silverek Photography

ABOVE: Although the Russians at Fort Ross introduced the Gravenstein apple to the region, it was orchardist Nathaniel Griffith who proved that the Gravenstein was a viable commercial crop, establishing the nearby Gold Ridge region as their rightful home. The industry soon grew, providing jobs in packing houses like the Apple Co-op Packing House in Forestville. Courtesy, Don Silverek Photography

ABOVE: *To promote their star crop, Sebastopol ranchers organized the first Gravenstein Apple Show in 1910. Sebastopol Mayor James P. Kelly kicked off the speeches, introducing the guest of honor, California Governor James Gillet. Music concessions and "riding devices" entertained the crowd until midnight. A confetti fight concluded the event on the final evening. Courtesy, Don Silverek Photography*

RIGHT: *Luther Burbank was well known for his development of many new varieties of plants and flowers. After 1875 he conducted his work in Sonoma County; he is pictured here in his garden at his Santa Rosa home. Courtesy, Don Silverek Photography*

FACING PAGE: *Sebastopol was, and still is, the world capital of the Gravenstein apple. Gravensteins were first introduced to the region by the Russians at Fort Ross. Orchardist Nathaniel Griffith planted Gravensteins near Sebastopol in the 1880s and was the first to introduce them as a viable commercial crop. To promote their star crop, Sebastopol ranchers organized the first Gravenstein Apple Show in 1910. Models built of apples were the highlight of the 1911 show, such as this all-apple model of the steam-powered paddlewheeler, the* Gold. *Courtesy, Sonoma County Museum*

families and a Jewish community center.

In 1910 Petaluma shipped 7 million dozen eggs to San Francisco. Production hit a peak in 1929 and then slumped, but in 1940 Petaluma shipped out 30 million dozen eggs, not far behind the record high of the 1920s. Petaluma also had the distinction of having a drug store devoted entirely to chickens. The Chicken Pharmacy, founded in 1929 by James Keyes, at one time dispensed 50,000 pullet pills a day. The store was featured in a 1939 issue of the *National Geographic*.

If Petaluma was the world's egg capital, Sebastopol was the world capital of the apple, or at least the Gravenstein apple. Fort Ross's Russians introduced "Gravs" to

Sonoma County, but it was orchardist Nathaniel Griffith in the 1880s who first planted Gravensteins in the Gold Ridge section. He proved the apple was practical as a commercial crop, earning himself the nickname "Grandfather of the Gravenstein."

By 1910, the year of the first Gravenstein Apple Show, Sebastopol had a population of 2,000 and the surrounding Gold Ridge district, with its rich, sandy soil, was devoted to apple orchards. Gravensteins ship well and ripen early. Growers picked in July and shipped the fruit to eastern markets. "We have no authentic proof to give, that the Garden of Eden was located in the Gold Ridge Region," wrote Anna Morrison Reed, editor of Petaluma's

Northern Crown magazine, "but it looks reasonable that it might have been since it is now a Paradise of orchards and homes."

The Gravenstein Apple Fair was a prime force in promoting the tart apples. In 1910, the year of the first apple fair, there were 5,700 acres planted in apples. By 1920 the county boasted 27,000 acres in apples. In the midst of the Depression Sonoma County was still shipping 50,000 tons of dried apples and 1.5 million boxes of fresh apples annually.

Growers made sure the second annual Gravenstein fair, held in 1911, was even more of an extravaganza than the first one. The electric railway offered special rates to Sebastopol, where concert bands and a "Great Midway" entertained the crowds. Japanese orchardists constructed a replica of the "Mikado's Palace" built entirely of apples. Famed horticulturist Luther Burbank kicked off the fair by pressing an electric button that lit up the pavilion and set the industrial exhibits in motion. "The Gravenstein apple has, above all others, proved to be the money winner in Sonoma County," commented Burbank, who had an experimental farm on the outskirts of Sebastopol. "It cannot be raised successfully in the hot valleys of Southern California. Sonoma County seems to be its home."

Burbank, the wizard of plant breeding, was the image of the practical American genius. Like Thomas Edison, who visited Burbank's garden in 1915, Burbank had remarkable persistence and an uncanny talent for perceiving the results of his experiments. A master of the empirical rather than the theoretical, Burbank contributed to the world of horticulture by inventing more than 800 new varieties of plants.

Born in Massachusetts in 1849, Burbank grew up on a farm. After high school he was largely self-taught, influenced in particular by Charles Darwin's *The Variation of Animals and Plants Under Domestication*. At age 21 he bought a farm in Massachusetts and embarked on a

55-year career of experimentation, finding his first fame with the "Burbank potato." In 1875 Burbank traded the rights to his potato for a ticket to Sonoma County, where he spent the remainder of his life devising new strains of plants on his farms in Santa Rosa and Sebastopol. Burbank achieved notoriety for sensational discoveries like the white blackberry and spineless cactus, which was a big hit at the 1908 Cloverdale Citrus Fair. But Burbank's less publicized work was more significant: he developed more than 100 new varieties of prunes and plums, 50 types of lilies, and 10 varieties of commercial berries.

Burbank's celebrated wizardry lay in keen observation of the differences between plants he was breeding. He turned the diversity of nature to his advantage, encouraging some traits and weeding out others, to create entirely new strains of plants. His guest book was a catalog of the world's celebrities, and his restored house and garden in Santa Rosa across from Juilliard Park are still popular attractions. Never was so much practical genius assembled in one place as on October 11, 1915, when Thomas Edison, Harvey Firestone, and Henry Ford, visiting the West Coast for the Panama-Pacific International Exposition, made a detour to walk the garden paths with Burbank.

Author Jack London spoke for his fellow visitors when he wrote in Burbank's guest book, "I'd rather do what you're doing than be Roosevelt, Rockefeller, King Edward or the Kaiser rolled into one."

London, another Sonoma County celebrity in his own time, dabbled in some farming of his own near Glen Ellen in the Valley of the Moon, where he settled in 1910 on a spread he named the Beauty Ranch. There he delved into experimental farming with the same intensity he brought to all his endeavors, designing and building a concrete "piggery" for raising hogs. "I go into farming because my philosophy and research have taught me to recognize the fact that a return to the soil is the basis of economics," he wrote. "Do you realize that I devote two hours a day to writing and ten to farming?"

Of all Sonoma County's authors past and present, none is more widely read than London, whose own life was an adventure yarn as colorful as his books. Born in 1876, he spent his teens sailing San Francisco Bay as an oyster pirate. Handsome, confident, and charismatic, he hurled himself into life's experiences. He traveled the country on freight trains as a hobo; signed on as an able-bodied seaman for Japan and the Bering Sea; and joined the Alaska gold rush of 1897 as a prospector in the Klondike.

OPPOSITE: Well-known American author Jack London chose to settle in Sonoma County in his later years. London was born in San Francisco and at the age of 17 shipped as a seaman to Japan and the Bering Sea. He later became a newspaper correspondent during the Russo-Japanese war and a war correspondent in Mexico. His stories had begun to appear in magazines when The Son of the Wolf *was published in 1900. Courtesy, Don Silverek Photography*

BELOW: While Jack London was well known for his many books and writings, many did not know that he had an interest in livestock. He raised pigs on his ranch in the Valley of the Moon. Pictured here is the "Piggery," the stone pig barn designed by London. Courtesy, Don Silverek Photography

ABOVE: Thomas Lake Harris, the first of the Utopians in Sonoma County, established his 1,400-acre Fountaingrove colony just north of Santa Rosa. The community was a prosperous one, with a book press and winery. Harris began his "Brotherhood of the New Life" in New York State and moved to his "new Eden of the West" in 1875. As the commune's last survior, Japanese nobleman Kanay Nagasawa inherited the estate, but anti-alien laws prevented Nagasawa from leaving Fountaingrove to his heirs. Baron Nagasawa appears here with relatives at Fountaingrove Ranch. Courtesy, Sonoma County Museum

London quit school at 14, but he haunted the Oakland Public Library and was largely self-taught. After his Alaskan adventures he found a market for his adventure novel *Son of the Wolf* (1900), followed by an outpouring of 50 books—novels, memoirs, ballads, and stories. Having experienced a childhood of intense poverty, London became a life-long crusader against exploitation, an ardent socialist who typically signed his letters, "Yours for the revolution." Like many celebrities, he essentially created himself, and the self he created was the Proletarian Hero who rose from nothing through hard work.

Although he was at one time the highest paid author in the country, London's schemes were always more grandiose than his royalties, and he wrote constantly to stay ahead of his debts. At the Beauty Ranch London and his wife, Charmian, designed Wolf House, a three-story mansion of wood and stone, but days before its completion someone torched the house. London never fully recovered from the setback. His health declined, aggravated by overindulgence in food and drink, until he died in 1916. The ruins of Wolf House remain in Jack London State Park, not far from the House of Happy Walls, built by Charmian as a tribute to Jack.

Sonoma County, with its fertile valleys and gentle climate, had all the prerequisites of "heaven on earth," attracting many utopians in the nineteenth century who dreamed of establishing ideal communities. In the late 1800s, of nine established communes in California, four were in Sonoma County.

The first of the religious and social reformers to put down roots in the county was Thomas Lake Harris, who

built his 1,400-acre Fountaingrove colony just north of Santa Rosa. Preaching a combination of Christianity and spiritualism, Harris began the Brotherhood of the New Life in New York State, then moved to his "new Eden of the West" in 1875. The community was a prosperous one, with a book press and winery. The wine was not only a financial success, but Harris believed the Fountaingrove vintage, made in the spirit of devotion, was infused with the "substance of Divine and celestial energy." Harris encouraged wealthy followers to pour assets into the communal coffers. These financial arrangements, combined with Harris' arcane views about sex and mysticism, eventually proved to be his undoing. Two visitors claimed Harris made sexual advances to them and made slaves of his fol-

ABOVE: Schools were usually named for the district in which they were located. These children are taking time out for exercise and relaxation in front of the Freestone District School. Note some of the students are barefoot. Courtesy, the Ray Van Skyke Collection

OPPOSITE, TOP: Parades were a major source of entertainment at the turn of the century. There was no end to the imagination invested in parade floats, such as this one seen in front of the courthouse and the Bank of Italy in Santa Rosa. Courtesy, Don Silverek Photography

ABOVE: The All American Sport was enjoyed by young people very early in the settlement of the county. These young men are representatives of Petaluma's 1905 high school baseball team. Courtesy, Sonoma County Museum

OPPOSITE: Athletics were an important part of school life. The Santa Rosa High School track team posed in their uniforms in 1901. Courtesy, Sonoma County Museum

lowers. They touched off a campaign of innuendo in the press that drove Harris from Fountaingrove in 1892.

Kanay Nagasawa, a Japanese nobleman, was the eventual heir to the Fountaingrove legacy. As a boy he and 14 other sons of nobles were smuggled out of Japan to learn the ways of the West, despite the ban on travel in or out of Japan. The others all returned to become leaders of westernized Japan, but Nagasawa joined Harris and remained at Fountaingrove all his life. As the commune's last surviving member, he inherited the estate and reigned as the Baron of Fountaingrove until his death in 1934. It was Nagasawa who built the "Round Barn," now one of Santa Rosa's landmarks. An accomplished viticulturalist, he traded advice with Luther Burbank and encouraged rapport between his adopted country and Japan, especially his home province of Kagoshima. Today Sonoma County's

Friends of Kagoshima maintain a cordial exchange with their counterparts in Japan.

French Utopians interested in social rather than religious reform began the Icaria Speranza commune south of Cloverdale in 1881. The 55 members, all French speakers, worked together in fields and vineyards, hoping to abolish inequality by holding goods in common. Within a few years debts from previous Icarian farms swamped the Sonoma County commune. Armand Dehay, writing to fel-

low Icarian Alexis Marchand, lamented, "My heart is broken to see that our Commune collapsed like a house built on sand."

The Altrurians launched another short-lived communal experiment in 1894. Enthused by the novel *A Traveler from Altruria* by William Dean Howell, which fused Christian morality with socialism, the members chipped in $50 apiece to found an ethical community on a 185-acre parcel on Mark West Creek. Altruria boasted a weaving operation and print shop; it had grandiose plans for a quarry and a hotel. Idealism and prosperity aren't necessarily mutually exclusive, but they were in Altruria's case. Perpetually in the red, the Altrurians amicably went their separate ways in 1895.

The fourth commune was not a deliberate colony but a group of devotees who clustered around the magnet-

ic Madame Emily Preston at her ranch north of Cloverdale. A renowned herbalist, Madame Preston prescribed salves, potions, and doses of her own elderberry wine. Easterners came to see her at the Preston Ranch or at a San Francisco apartment she kept for consultations. Patients believed she could diagnose them by looking into their eyes, and 100 followers became so attached to her that they stayed permanently. She allowed them to build on her land for free and pick fruit from her orchards. Madame Preston's religious code consisted of straightforward pronouncements like, "Condemn no church. Have no discord. Strive for unity." A writer for the *San Francisco Chronicle* in 1887 commented on her influence: "Her hallucination, if it be a hallucination, has a tendency only to elevate." When she died in 1909, aged 90, the *Cloverdale Reveille* called her "a much beloved woman."

A Rose Carnival and parade restored Santa Rosans' post-earthquake spirits in the spring of 1907. The traditional Rose Carnival, heralding the awakening of the sleeping earth from the long dormant winter, has been a tradition since the 1800s and features roses and spring blossoms in its events and parade. Children were the primary participants in the parade. These young girls displaying new dresses and glowing smiles are Alice Cullin, Claire Coltrin, Margaret Forsythe, and Zelma Carithers. Courtesy, Sonoma County Library

Quake to 1940

It was a quiet Wednesday morning, 5:13 a.m., in Santa Rosa. Travelers at the Occidental Hotel and the Saint Rose were still asleep, and out on the street paper boys were making their rounds. Forty-eight seconds later, on the morning of April 18, 1906, virtually every business in downtown Santa Rosa was in ruins and most of the homes were damaged.

Although the quake is known as the Great San Francisco Earthquake, no city suffered as much damage proportionally as Santa Rosa. The next day a joint edition of three San Francisco newspapers—the *Call, Chronicle,* and *Examiner*—carried a story announcing, "Santa Rosa Is a Total Wreck." While some Sonoma County towns stand on stable bedrock, Santa Rosa was built on loose deposits of alluvium that shook like jello. The entire downtown section collapsed in a pile of loose bricks. The 2,000-seat Athenaeum theatre was a shambles, and the four-story courthouse with its impressive dome collapsed like a fallen wedding cake. Inside the Presbyterian Church on Humboldt, the massive chandelier swayed and fell, crushing empty seats that had been full of worshippers three mornings before on Easter Sunday. The town's water system was in ruins, dooming the Santa Rosa Fire Department's efforts to combat the resulting blazes.

Over 100 people died in Santa Rosa, many in the collapse of the town's three large hotels, the Occidental, the Saint Rose, and the Grand. "They fell as if constructed of playing cards, and in the heaps were buried the hundreds of lodgers," reported the San Francisco papers. The Sonoma County Library has a microfilm copy of a *Press Democrat* delivered minutes before the cataclysm; someone scrawled across the top of the front page, "The boy who handled this paper was killed in the quake."

Damage was widespread. The new Masonic Hall in Windsor was destroyed. The towns of Tomales and Bloomfield were in ruins. Three workers at the Great Eastern quicksilver mine near Guerneville were crushed by falling rocks, and in Occidental brick chimneys tumbled from every roof in town. La Bonita Hotel in Duncans Mills crumpled to the ground, and the Fort Ross chapel, built directly over the San Andreas Fault, collapsed. The entire Point Reyes peninsula jumped 17 feet northward, knocking the Point Reyes lighthouse off its mount and upsetting the delicate mechanism of the revolving Fresnel lens. Out at sea the skipper of the *Alliance,* steaming past Eureka, felt the sudden jolt and thought his ship had run aground.

In San Francisco, most damage was done by fires that swept the city after the earthquake. Firefighting was hampered by ruptured water mains. Sonoma County winemakers learned their vast warehouses in the city were destroyed. Winemaker Charles Bundschu, writing to a friend days after the quake, lamented, "Our building fell at 5 o'clock on the first day. When we got the news, my tears fell incessantly . . . It meant the labor and struggle of two generations, and now—and now?" Italian-Swiss Colony was luckier. The quake ruined 10 million gallons of wine but the warehouse near Telegraph Hill was saved from fire because of a natural spring underneath. For several days the "lake" at the Italian-Swiss warehouse was one of the chief sources of fresh water in the city.

Towns with less damage sent help to Santa Rosa. Petaluma's Elks Lodge and its chamber of commerce each sent a carload of provisions. Sebastopol sent a fire engine. On Sunday the Fitch family rode in with a wagonload of provisions from Calistoga's Red Cross Society. The Northwestern Pacific Railroad offered its wrecking crew with a derrick and steam shovel to clear away the debris of downtown.

Santa Rosans were quick to dust themselves off and carry on with their lives. The Sunday after the quake, Presbyterians carried their chairs and reed organ to a vacant lot behind the church and held outdoor services. The following day students returned to the Santa Rosa Business College, and workers were erecting a temporary city hall on the Native Sons' lot on Mendocino Avenue. Within a week the *Press Democrat* leased a lot on Mendocino formerly occupied by a Chinese washhouse and started on a new building. Paul Hahman's ledger, with entries written in his elegant script, shows business at his drug store was interrupted for only two days. Hahman's Apothecary had the first plate glass window in Santa Rosa's new downtown. Local newspapers, once started printing makeshift editions, were full of news about mercantile ventures rising from the ashes. Much of the stock of businesses like Mailer's Hardware and Bacigalupi's Grocery had been saved. Within a week most Fourth Street merchants set up shop at home or in temporary quarters. Train cars full of brick and lumber arrived to construct the new improved Santa Rosa.

City fathers, mustering as much optimism as anyone could under the circumstances, looked on the disaster as a kind of unplanned urban renewal. "For a long time it has been generally recognized that the majority of Santa Rosa's business streets were too narrow, and now that the opportunity for widening them has arrived it must be embraced," reasoned an April 30 editorial in the jointly issued *Santa Rosa Democrat-Republican.* "It will only be a few years until electric cars are occupying all our principal streets . . ."

The city council, convening two days after the disaster, announced its intentions to "Build a bigger and better Santa Rosa." A *Press Democrat* editorial on April 23 commented on the need for a new courthouse, adding, "While we are about it, we might as well build it right. A modern up-to-date structure is the only thing that will fill the bill." The quake had destroyed nineteenth-century Santa Rosa; a twentieth-century town rose from the rubble.

Even before the quake, Sonoma County residents had felt the tremors of a different kind of upheaval: the social reform movement that discouraged drinking. Defenders of saloons saw them as social clubs for the working man; reformers condemned them as part of a cycle of crime and poverty. An unlikely opponent of dry laws was Anna Morrison Reed, editor of Petaluma's *Northern Crown* magazine. A supporter of social reform and a founding member of the Pacific Coast Women's Press Association, Reed nevertheless toured the country lecturing against prohibition. "The whole world is, at this time undergoing an agitation, and attempted reform, at the hands of 'professed moralists,'" Reed wrote in her magazine in 1916. "Any attempted national prohibition . . . would result in a practical failure, because all experience demonstrates that the mass of the people will not tolerate such regulation." Reed also brought up an argument that carried plenty of weight in Sonoma County. Alcohol was big business. Eight hundred wineries in California were in jeopardy, as were the state's 60 breweries that used 80,000 pounds of barley and over a million pounds of hops a year. Sonoma County, heavily depen-

dent on grapes and hops, faced economic disaster.

The call to ban alcohol gained momentum after 1900; by 1917 two-thirds of the states had adopted individual prohibition laws. During World War I Congress banned the sale of intoxicants to conserve grain supplies and then drafted an Eighteenth Amendment to the U.S. Constitution barring sale and manufacture of alcoholic beverages. The states quickly ratified it and Congress passed the Volstead Act to enforce it. Comic Will Rogers summed up the contradictions of the years to follow: "If you think this country ain't dry, just watch 'em vote. If you think this country ain't wet, just watch 'em drink. You see when they vote it's counted, but when they drink it ain't."

Prohibition began in January 1920. A January 16 *Press Democrat* headline announced that "John Barleycorn Is Breathing His Last Here Today." On the first Sunday of the dry era, parishioners at St. Rose's Catholic Church in Santa Rosa were startled by the week's selection from holy scripture. It was the passage from the Gospel of John telling how Jesus turned water into wine for the wedding guests at Cana.

Locally, winemakers wondered what to do with three million gallons of wine, stored in Sonoma County vats, which could not legally be sold or moved. Librarians puz-

zled over whether to whisk books on winemaking off the shelves. One thing soon became apparent: people would exercise their imaginations to get around the new law.

The Volstead Act permitted citizens to make 200 gallons for home use, so there was still a market for grapes. In fact, by 1930 cultivation of grapes actually rose to 30,000 acres. But times were hard for wineries; between 1920 and 1933, when the act was repealed, Sonoma County lost two-thirds of its more than 200 wineries. The Bundschu family closed its winery and harvested grapes for others. Sebastiani's in Sonoma survived by concentrating on medicinal and sacramental wines, which were legal, and by shipping

OPPOSITE, TOP: The dome of the Sonoma County courthouse collapsed in the great earthquake of 1906. Courtesy, Don Silverek Photography

OPPOSITE, BOTTOM: The earthquake of 1906 dealt a devastating blow to what had seemed to be sound structures, including the Santa Rosa Free Public Library, which was constructed of stone. Courtesy, Sonoma County Museum

BELOW: San Francisco's newspapers estimated the 1906 earthquake death toll in Santa Rosa would be in the thousands. Fortunately, this was not true. The actual count of lives lost in Santa Rosa was 103—many of them were lodgers in Santa Rosa's three largest hotels. Pictured is the coroner's wagon waiting for victims to be pulled from the ruins of the Occidental Hotel in Santa Rosa. Courtesy, Sonoma County Museum

grapes back east to home winemakers. Italian-Swiss Colony made grape drinks and printed a pamphlet, "Is Entertaining a Lost Art?," to promote them. The pamphlet will "undoubtedly fill a need and make one realize that after all things are not 'as dark as they seem,'" the winemakers wistfully wrote. The booklet (preserved in the California Historical Society Library) included recipes for wine jelly and offered dining advice such as serving "Riesling type" beverages with oysters.

Saloons closed their doors and reopened as restaurants and stores. Some breweries, like Brandt's in Healdsburg, folded during Prohibition. Others, like Santa Rosa's

Grace Brothers, weathered the dry era as ice houses and bottling plants. Ranchers continued to grow hops; the crop's banner year was 1931 with 21,000 acres of hops planted in Sonoma County. Sonoma County beer drinkers weren't left high and dry. "During Prohibition everybody had their own little hop patches and made beer," remembered George Proctor, whose family owned seven hop ranches and at one time controlled half the hops in the state. "People drank more during Prohibition than they do now."

The county had its share of bootleggers and clandestine hooch. One local minister lamented that Sonoma

County was "wet, very wet." He urged his flock to dry out and wring the alcohol out of the rest of the community, too, by informing if need be. A tip led lawmen to one of their biggest busts in April 1931, when Sheriff Mike Flohr, District Attorney Emmett Donohue, and a small posse burst in on a distilling operation near the Laguna. Three surprised moonshiners left the boilers going full tilt and made a getaway in a rowboat. When the lawmen fired a few shots in the air, the trio leapt from the boat and scrambled away through the Laguna's knee-high muddy water. The posse nabbed two bootleggers but the third escaped, leaving behind his muddy trousers. The sheriff confiscated a thousand gallons of alcohol, 30,000 gallons of ferment-

By the start of the 1930s, the national mood had shifted. President Herbert Hoover was staunchly behind Prohibition, but his 1932 challenger, Franklin Roosevelt, was just as strongly against it. FDR's election was closely followed by repeal of Prohibition. "We voted for Roosevelt in 1932 to get beer back and we got it," remembered "Babe" Wood, a third-generation hop rancher whose grandfather started one of the county's first ranches in the 1870s. Sonoma County hop ranchers, grape growers, and vintners toasted their renewed good fortune and got to work. Trucks from Grace Brothers Brewery rolled again, each with a banner proclaiming "Happy Days Are Here Again."

ing mash, 100 sacks of sugar, and the still.

Much of the illegal liquor was smuggled into the country. On the north coast, ships from Vancouver anchored offshore just outside the international limit. When darkness fell a small boat would speed a shipment onto the beaches or even right through the Golden Gate. Along the isolated Sonoma coast north of Jenner, the doghole ports once used for loading timber proved handy for unloading booze. When the coast highway from Jenner to Gualala was completed in the late 1920s, rumrunners could make quick trips to the city from smugglers' coves at Salt Point and present-day Sea Ranch.

ABOVE: The Pacific Telephone and Telegraph staff poses in front of their building in 1922, bringing communications to Sonoma County. Courtesy, Sonoma County Museum

OPPOSITE: Neighborhood movie theaters were the main source of entertainment before the advent of television. In addition to feature films, they offered live shows, newsreels, and cartoons. Santa Rosa had the Cline, the California, and the Roxy on B Street, the Strand on Davis Street, and the Elite and the Rose on Fourth Street. Admission in the 1940s was only 20 cents and popcorn was only five cents. Cash night at the California theater in Santa Rosa attracted throngs of people, as pictured in this photo. Courtesy, Sonoma County Library

"Babe" Wood constructed the building at the corner of Mendocino and Seventh in 1935 to house his REO truck franchise and later acquired DeSoto and Plymouth franchises. He eventually dropped Plymouth and acquired Pontiac and Cadillac, remaining in the same building from 1935 to 1976, when the dealership was moved to 2925 Corby Avenue, where it is still operating today. Courtesy, Sonoma County Library

But for hop growers the happy days were not to last. Beer was as popular as ever, but people preferred a lighter tasting brew. Hops, which gives beer its strong, bitter taste, was less in demand. Local ranchers also found it hard to compete with large-scale hop operations that sprang up in the Central Valley after World War II. The final blow to Sonoma County hop ranching was downy mildew. Coastal fog kept the hop vines too moist, and ranchers began to lose half their crops to the damp. By the 1960s hops, once a major Sonoma County crop, weren't profitable anymore. Grace Brothers Brewery shut down in the 1960s. Ranchers rolled with the times, converting their ranches to prune orchards and vineyards.

After Prohibition's repeal, county grape growers raised bulk wine grapes for bottlers outside the county. Small and medium-sized wineries popped up in Dry Creek, Alexander Valley, and along the Russian River. But the wine industry had suffered a setback. In Sonoma County, the grape harvest had peaked at 68,778 tons in 1910. In 1930 it had fallen to 33,934 tons a year, and 1940 saw only 29,425 tons of grapes produced. The wine industry would not fully recover until Americans turned whole-heartedly to wine drinking after the 1960s.

By the 1930s Americans had more to worry about than alcohol. The stock market crash of 1929 sent the world economy into a decade-long tailspin. Farmers from the drought-ravaged Dust Bowl migrated to California's valleys in hopes of work. FDR's New Deal, an alphabet soup of federal agencies designed to keep people working, funded many Sonoma County projects. A WPA (Works Progress Administration) grant paid Richard Brooks and Dorothy Wolf to conduct research on Sonoma County itself. After digging through archives and interviewing old timers, they wrote *Sonoma County: History and Description,* and *Foreign Born in Sonoma County,* a study of immigrants, both published by the WPA in 1936. The Public Works Administration kicked in half the money to put up a new firehouse in Santa Rosa. The WPA did $20,000 worth of work to prevent flooding on the Russian River and allocated $8,000 to spruce up the Sonoma County Fairgrounds with shrubbery and paint. Another New Deal brainchild was the CCC (Civilian Conservation Corps), an army of young men who earned $30 a month for forestry work and building projects ($25 went back home to their families). CCC boys lived in rural barracks resembling summer camps. They built bridges and walls as well as the amphitheater in Armstrong Woods. Materials were scarce so the camps often produced their own. "We had a pipe factory and made our own pipe, and did a lot of drainage work, too," remembers Marty Coorpender, a Santa Rosan who lived at Camp Sebastopol.

A major beneficiary of federal largesse was Santa Rosa Junior College, founded in 1918. The initial student body was 19, with eight faculty. At the time Santa Rosa had a population of 13,000 and boasted a high school, a junior high, and four grammar schools. For several years the junior college shared facilities with Santa Rosa High School. The college got its own Mendocino Avenue campus in 1931. The 40-acre site was originally earmarked as a park and was a favorite spot of Luther Burbank. Co-owners of the property, the city of Santa Rosa and the Santa Rosa Chamber of Commerce, agreed to locate SRJC there with a proviso for a 350-foot setback along Mendocino Avenue to preserve the park-like setting of oaks and flowers.

Santa Rosa Junior College was originally intended as an extension of UC Berkeley and had the same requirements, although in the 1930s its program expanded to encompass vocational training. Two early champions of the new school were Genevieve Mott and Clarence "Red" Tauzer. Mott was an English instructor in 1918, dean of women during the 1920s, and one of those most responsi-

ble for holding the school together in its early years. Tauzer, a graduate of Stanford Law School, coached football and basketball in the school's early years and served as perennial liaison between the college and the community. He was one of the school's biggest boosters until his death in 1948. Although the Depression meant hard times in general, it was the time of greatest expansion for the junior college. In 1938 Public Works Administration funds built three of the school's red brick, ivy-covered buildings —Analy Hall, Burbank Auditorium, and Bussman Hall— with a quarter-million-dollar bond.

Not all federal projects were so eagerly welcomed. When the Farm Security Administration planned to construct a model migrant workers' camp in Windsor in 1938,

These young men and women were students at the Santa Rosa Business College in the 1920s. Courtesy, Sonoma County Museum

county supervisors joined local farmers in loud objections. Housing for the laborers would be controlled not by the county but by the government, and that didn't sit well with local farmers and businessmen. Despite the objections, the government built Camp Windsor for 250 people, mostly Dust Bowl families in search of seasonal work.

The legacy of bad feeling between farm owners and farm workers stemmed partly from an ugly incident in 1935 when two union organizers were literally tarred and feathered. Farmers blamed labor organizers for fomenting a strike during the fruit and hop harvest, and early in August 1935 anti-labor toughs broke up a strike meeting at Santa Rosa's Germania Hall,

The female jurors in this June 1920 photo were the first women to sit on a jury in Sonoma County. Courtesy, Sonoma County Library

throwing the leaders out into the street. Two weeks later, labor leaders got wind that another meeting would be broken up, so they stayed home. As a result, frustrated anti-unionists broke up into small packs and rode to several spots around the county to kidnap the unionists, bringing them to a Santa Rosa warehouse. There they tarred and feathered Jack Green and Sol Nitzberg and threatened the rest. Green and Nitzberg told their woes to the Sonoma County Grand Jury, but the county district attorney declined to prosecute, citing lack of evidence. Then California Attorney General U.S. Webb, overriding local authorities, ordered the arrest of 23 prominent Sonoma County residents, including legionnaires, bankers, and the president and secretary of the Healdsburg Chamber of Commerce, on charges of kidnapping and assault. When a dozen of the men went to trial in October 1936, the courtroom was so packed even some of the defendants had to stand. The jury acquitted all parties after deliberating for 16 minutes. Business interests continued to blame outside agitators for the unrest, though Nitzberg was a Petaluma farmer and another victim was a Cotati rancher. Unionists in turn branded Sonoma County "a vigilante-infested area."

The "red purge" wasn't the only vigilante action in Sonoma County, though perhaps it was the last. The last

lynching in Sonoma County was in 1920, in the aftermath of the murder of a popular sheriff. Sonoma County Sheriff James Petray, assisted by two officers from the city, cornered three wanted members of San Francisco's Howard Street Gang in a Santa Rosa house. Shots rang out and when the dust cleared Petray and one other officer lay dead; the other died soon after. Petray's deputies nabbed "Spanish Charley" Valento, George Boyd, and Terry Fitts at the back door. Several dozen vigilantes liberated the men from the jail, took them to an isolated hillside, and hanged them. Public sympathy was solidly behind the vigilantes, and no one asked any penetrating questions. Rumors told of a party of 100 angry San Francisco policemen riding up to Santa Rosa and dispatching the thugs who had laid their comrades low. Decades later it came out that several dozen Sonoma County folks, mostly friends of Petray, carried out the lynching.

One event of the 1930s destined to have enormous impact on the Redwood Empire was the opening of the Golden Gate Bridge. People on both sides of the mile-wide Golden Gate, the opening to San Francisco Bay, had debated the building of such a span; many believed it impossible. The bridge remained in the realm of imagination until Frank Doyle, president of the Santa Rosa Chamber of Commerce, mustered North Bay supporters of a bridge at a meeting on January 13, 1923. One hundred delegates from 21 counties gathered at the Santa Rosa City Hall, and the Golden Gate Bridge Association emerged from that historic meeting. In 1930 the counties voted for $35 million in bonds to foot the bill, and construction began in 1932. On April 27, 1937, the driving of a golden rivet completed the steel-and-cement construction. Residents on both sides prepared for the party of the decade, a nine-day "Golden Gate Fiesta." On May 28, 1937, President Roosevelt pressed a button in the White House, activating the go-ahead signal at the bridge. San Francisco Mayor Angelo Rossi praised the span that "signalizes the closing, forever, of an age-old barrier to land travel." More than 31,500 cars crossed in the first 24 hours.

A special edition of the *San Francisco Examiner* announced that "the great Redwood Empire, drawn closer by the time-destroying link of the Golden Gate Bridge, scans the future with confidence and assurance in the heritage to come." The *Examiner* profiled Sonoma County, population 65,300, with its "world-famed Redwood Highway stretching away from the Golden Gate, beckoning the motorists on." The remark was a hint of traffic jams to come. The June 1 *Press Democrat* reported that at the end of Memorial Day weekend, "a solid double line of southbound cars was at a standstill as far north as Hamilton Field." Record crowds flooded Sonoma Valley and Russian River resorts, and hundreds ended up sleeping in their cars. Santa Rosans were on the hop pumping gas into an endless stream of cars. On the Fourth of July, 1937, the Russian River was a magnet for party-goers. Thousands of tourists filled the dance halls of Monte Rio and Guerneville "after traveling almost bumper to bumper across the Golden Gate Bridge and up the congested Redwood Highway," according to the *Press Democrat*. The Santa Rosa Chamber of Commerce met that week to discuss plans for a four-lane highway.

Tourists in autos were preceded by a generation that frequented Sonoma County resorts by train. After tracks were laid in the 1870s, Bay Area residents would hop on ferries and ride to Sonoma Valley or the Russian River. Farmers opened their houses and barns to boarders for the summer. Northwestern Pacific promoted North Bay hotels along its tracks in an annual "Vacationland" guidebook.

Sonoma Valley had dozens of destinations for tourists who came to hunt, fish, or "take the waters." Agua Caliente offered "the nearest hot sulphur springs to San Francisco." Boyes Hot Springs boasted 118-degree mineral baths and well-furnished tents and cottages. Northwestern Pacific's 1909 directory listed 20 hotels in Glen Ellen alone and many more in El Verano and Sonoma.

By the turn of the century, when the timber business was flagging on the lower Russian River, the tourist business was picking up steam. Sonoma County folks ran guest houses with two or three rooms, or built full-scale hotels for 100 or more. The Northwestern Pacific offered its popular "Triangle Trip": for $2.50 passengers could ride to the Russian River on the narrow gauge in the morning, spend an idyllic day among the redwoods, and return via the broad-gauge line in the afternoon (or else do the trip in reverse).

No single event brought more business to Sonoma County than the opening of the Golden Gate Bridge, and no one worked harder than Frank Doyle to see it built. The bridge was only a dream until 1923 when Doyle, then president of the Santa Rosa Chamber of Commerce, convened a meeting to spark interest in a bridge linking the North Bay with San Francisco. On May 28, 1937, Doyle was on hand to officially open the bridge that would flood the Redwood Empire with tourists and commerce. Two months earlier, Doyle was driven across the span, making him the first person to cross the Golden Gate by automobile. Courtesy, Exchange Bank

ABOVE: The Redwood Highway is seen as it passes through the heart of Santa Rosa's downtown business district. Courtesy, Don Silverek Photography

OPPOSITE, TOP: Trains were replaced by auto stages in the 1930s as the era of the railroad was surpassed by the automobile age. Courtesy, Don Silverek Photography

OPPOSITE, BOTTOM: Cigarettes became big business for jobbers in the 1920s and 1930s. The truck pictured here is making a delivery in the Railroad Square area of Santa Rosa. Courtesy, Don Silverek Photography

Resorts flourished along the tracks at Mirabel, Hilton, Rio Nido, Guerneville, Guernewood Park, Monte Rio, Cazadero, Camp Meeker, and Occidental. Accommodations on the Russian River ranged from floored tents to multi-storied hotels nestled among the redwoods. Sully's Resort, for instance, sent its autobus to the Monte Rio train station to collect guests, who stayed for $20 a week in the four-story hotel or in tent cottages for a bit less. According to Sully's 1912 brochure, Monte Rio had "all the usual amusements, large dance halls, boxball alleys, moving pictures, billiards and pool," not to mention canoeing and basking on sandy beaches. The Monte Rio Hotel, showpiece of downtown Monte Rio in the 1910s and 1920s, had a unique claim to fame: each of its seven stories had a ground floor entrance. (The hotel was built against the side of a steep slope.) Hotel Rusticano in Camp Meeker advertised croquet, tennis, bowling, and dancing. M.C. "Boss" Meeker also divvied up land and sold $20 lots; for another $100 the buyer could have a cottage built. Hundreds of people bought lots from Forestville to Duncans Mills and built summer homes.

Tourism was not enough to sustain the cost of running a railroad. Timber in the Russian River area was already becoming depleted when a devastating fire in 1923 swept along the river from Guerneville all the way to the sea, destroying mills and trees. The cost of repairing aging trestles and equipment was also becoming prohibitive. By the 1920s automobiles were becoming the transportation of choice, and a new paved road linking Guerneville with the Redwood Highway was completed in 1927. Northwestern Pacific first abandoned its narrow-gauge line; as the last train pulled out of Occidental in 1930, townspeople sadly placed a banner on the train that read, "Gone, But Not Forgotten." An autobus took its place. The broad-gauge line to Guerneville saw its final run on November 14, 1935. Everyone in Guerneville took a day off and hopped on board with lunches and beer; as the train left Monte Rio for the last time, the volunteer fire department turned their sirens on full blast in farewell.

The end of the railroads to the Russian River was not the end of tourism. During the 1930s and 1940s young people flocked to Russian River resorts for nightly dances. Dance halls at Mirabel

Park, Guernewood Village, and the Grove in Guerneville booked bands to play all summer. Ray Tellier and his 15-piece orchestra played the Grove all during the '30s, and Reg Code brought his collegiate band from UC Berkeley to the Guernewood Bowl. Big bands came up to play one-night stands at Rio Nido. Ozzie Nelson's band played Rio Nido in the late '30s (Harriet was the lead singer), and the sounds of Benny Goodman's clarinet bounced off the canyon walls. There were good times as the 1930s drew to an end and the Depression loosened its grip, but in Europe and Asia, the war that would engulf the world had already begun.

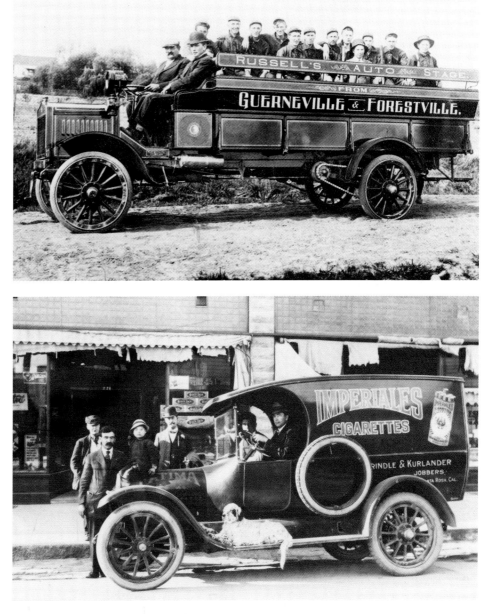

In the 1930s Santa Rosa was still a small town, but Sonoma County ranked 10th in agricultural prowess among all the counties of the nation. The Sonoma County Fair was organized in 1936 to celebrate the county's produce and livestock. The first fair operated on a budget of $50,000, and charged 50 cents for admission. Courtesy, Sonoma County Library

The Challenge of Expansion

In 1941 Europe had been at war for two years, and the U.S. and Japan seemed headed for conflict, but on the Pacific coast, World War II caught everyone off guard. With the news of Japan's attack on Pearl Harbor on December 7, 1941, coast residents suddenly braced themselves for possible invasion. The following day army troops hurried to Tomales and Bodega Head to keep watch in hastily erected watchtowers. Ammunition was in such short supply that the man on guard duty gave his ammo to the next man coming on watch.

Troops and civilians scrambled to prepare a defense, especially after Japanese planes were spotted near San Francisco. The December 9 *Press Democrat* headline warned "Enemy Here," and Santa Rosa station KSRO shut down for several hours to prevent enemy aircraft from homing in on radio beams. Three days after Pearl Harbor, 1,200 infantrymen of the 7th Division were guarding Sonoma County from their new regimental headquarters at the county fairgrounds. Air raid wardens set up posts at strategic points like Mount Saint Helena and Mount Jackson. Attorney Red Tauzer organized 96 volunteers, mostly World War I veterans, into a unit of the state home guards in Santa Rosa. "What impressed me the most was the lack of any hysteria on the part of the men," Tauzer said. "It was a cool, clear-thinking group of American citizens."

The Santa Rosa City Council passed a blackout ordinance; one long siren blast meant "lights out." Blackout curtains went up every night all over the county. During the second blackout, on December 11, twins born to the Erwin family of Petaluma at Sonoma County Hospital were heralded as "the blackout babies."

The first tragic news came by telegram a week after Pearl Harbor. William Montgomery, a 20-year-old Navy gunner's mate from Santa Rosa, had been killed. By war's end, 243 such telegrams would come to Sonoma County homes. But there were also lucky escapes. Ensign Kenneth Eymann (later a Sonoma County Superior Court judge) was feared lost on the USS *West Virginia* at Pearl Harbor but was later found safe, away from his ship on a pass.

Wartime precautions became routine. In Bodega Bay, the Coast Guard took over the Bay Hotel and patrolled Doran and Salmon Creek beaches with dogs. Tank crews, stationed at the former CCC camp east of

Freestone, regularly rolled through Bodega Bay on the way to maneuvers at Bodega Dunes. Bodega Bay became a guinea pig for camouflage experiments; longtime resident Glenice Carpenter remembers planes flying overhead and blanketing the town several times with smokescreen. Carpenter also recalls deafening sounds of a battle somewhere off Bodega Bay early in the war. The shaking from the offshore barrage was so intense that her father, who ran the Bay Hotel, hustled his customers outside. "The hotel was a rather old building, and we got out and stood in the street," Carpenter said. "We were afraid the building would fall down." The battle was never officially reported; residents suspect a Japanese submarine was intercepted near shore.

The war era brought a number of projects that would later serve peacetime uses. The airport long envisioned by county planners came to life when the Civil Aeronautics Authority provided $300,000 for a site on Laughlin Road northwest of Santa Rosa. Army interceptor squadrons practiced on the field that would later become the Sonoma County Airport. At Santa Rosa Junior College, enrollment plummeted from approximately 1,000 students to 235. But the war meant eventual expansion for SRJC. The nursing program began in 1942, and by 1943 the school housed 750 men of the Army Special Training Program. New barracks later became student housing.

While ranchers' sons were fighting in Europe and the Pacific, German soldiers were picking hops in the Russian River Valley. Camp Windsor, originally built for migrant workers during the Depression, housed 200 to 300 German prisoners, mostly captured submarine crewmen. The German POWs left their minimum security prison each morning and goosestepped out to the orchards and hop fields, singing German songs. The friendly, hard-working POWs were a big hit with local ranchers, who threw a farewell beer and pretzel party for them when the war ended.

Japanese residents of Sonoma County, most of them native born, didn't fare as well. To allay suspicions against their community, 100 members of the county's Japanese American Citizen's League met in Petaluma and drafted a statement condemning Japan for its "unprovoked attack upon the Hawaiian Islands and American possessions in the Pacific." Despite such avowals of loyalty, on February

19, 1942, President Roosevelt signed Executive Order 9066, calling for the removal of Japanese from military areas, which included most of California. The county's 758 Japanese residents—550 of them born here and therefore U.S. citizens—braced for relocation. On May 11, 1942, the order came giving "all persons of Japanese ancestry" four days to sell or store their businesses and belongings. Homes, apple dryers, and poultry farms were hurriedly sold or leased. Many sold off chicks and livestock at 10 percent of market value. On May 16 and 17, with only as much as they could carry, they boarded the train in Santa Rosa and Petaluma, bound for a staging area in Merced. From there, most Sonoma County internees went to barracks in Colorado like Camp Amache, where they lived until the order was rescinded in December 1944.

Some came home to find their businesses in good order. Others, like Sebastopol apple rancher Joe Furusho, found renters had failed to keep up mortgage payments or set aside an agreed-upon share of profits. Some had friends like Lea and Joseph Perry of Sebastopol, who ran their own apple dryer but looked after the farms of neighbors they felt had been unjustly exiled. Most of those who returned to Sonoma County recovered their farms but lost the income from the war years.

At the end of World War II, American GI's came home, ready for life to return to normal. For soldiers from rural counties like Sonoma, that meant returning to small communities surrounded by farms. Even Santa Rosa and Petaluma, Sonoma's population hubs, were relatively small. In 1940, Santa Rosa had 12,605 people; Petaluma was second with 8,034. The other cities were smaller: Healdsburg with 2,507, Sebastopol with 1,856, Cloverdale with 1,292, Sonoma with 1,158

Hop pickers at Ballard Ranch, 1940s. High school girls were recruited to get the crops in while men were away in the armed forces. Courtesy, Sonoma County Museum

Autumn brings brilliant hues of yellow and red to the vines of the Sonoma County wine country's 150 grape growers. The area's 11 micro-climates add variety to the county's many wine offerings. Photo by John Elk III

ABOVE: "Plant Wizard" Luther Burbank lived and worked on the grounds in Santa Rosa that today bear his name. The famous horticulturist developed more than 800 varieties of plants, including hundreds of flowers. The Luther Burbank Home and Gardens is a popular Santa Rosa tourist destination. Photo by Patty Salkeld

LEFT: A couple and their dog enjoy a lakeside picnic with several mallards at the Hop Kiln Winery in Healdsburg. Photo by Patty Salkeld

OPPOSITE: Along the placid Russian River, a stand of Monterey Cypresses is illuminated by the late afternoon sun in this view from Highway 116 near Duncans Mills. Photo by Patty Salkeld

ABOVE: Agriculture is Sonoma County's prime industry. Here, sheep graze at a farm on the Sonoma County coast. Photo by Kerrick James

OPPOSITE: Mission San Francisco Solano, founded by Padre Jose Altamira in 1823, was the last and northernmost Franciscan mission of Alta California. It is commonly known as Sonoma Mission. Photo by Patty Salkeld

ABOVE: Evoking images of early California, two young men look for a place to hitch their horses while stopping for a bite at Von Sydow's Grocery Deli on East Napa Street in Sonoma in the mid '80s. Photo by Patty Salkeld.

LEFT: A mother and child bask in the early afternoon sun on a swing-set at Sonoma Plaza in the town of Sonoma. Photo by Patty Salkeld.

OPPOSITE: Sonoma County's charm is due in large part to its small towns and older buildings. The Sonoma Hotel on Spain Street in the town of Sonoma typifies the area's quaintness. Photo by Patty Salkeld

The sun sets behind a sheep-grazing hill in Occidental in this serene view from Coleman Valley Road. Photo by Patty Salkeld

and Cotati with 1,000. Geyserville, Kenwood, Forestville, and Guerneville had a few hundred each.

But the war had set in motion forces that would transform California into a population magnet for the rest of the country. The state's two metropolitan areas, the Bay area and the Los Angeles basin, mushroomed with wartime industry. The war in the Pacific had also given tens of thousands of soldiers and sailors a glimpse of the Golden State and its fabulous climate. Many of them grabbed their discharge papers and headed to the West Coast. The state's population jumped from 6.9 million in 1940 to 10.5 million in 1950 and kept climbing; by the end of the millennium, California would swell to 34 million people.

Sonoma County missed the heavy industrialization that transformed Oakland and other cities lining San Francisco Bay during the war, but the advent of peacetime sparked an unprecedented building spree that spilled over into the Bay Area's rural counties. Perhaps no one is more responsible for Sonoma County's postwar growth than Hugh B. Codding. A Navy Seabee during World War II, Codding came back to his home-

The Leghorns were the pride of Petaluma in the '40s and '50s. Many of the players were hometown boys, who formed the semi-pro team after they returned home from World War II. They pitted themselves against local rivals like the Santa Rosa Bonecrushers and the San Francisco Windbreakers and ended their season with the annual Egg Bowl. Courtesy, Sonoma County Museum

Jim Miyano spent much of World War II with his family in a relocation camp at Camp Amache, Colorado. Before the war he went out for football and track at Petaluma High School; after the war he was a rancher and commercial fisherman. Courtesy, Miyano family

town of Santa Rosa in 1945 with $400 and boundless ambition. In the early 1950s, he founded the community of Montgomery Village (named after Billy Montgomery, the first Santa Rosan killed in the war) and built 3,000 homes just east of Santa Rosa, earning a reputation as the boy wonder of California construction. While *Life* photographers looked on, the flamboyant Codding built a church, steeple and all, in five hours. He later put up a house in three hours, nine minutes.

County building codes were sketchier in those days, but with the demand for veterans' housing, Codding found himself constructing homes to Federal Housing Administration specifications. The FHA required steel reinforcement, a precaution Codding considered unnecessary. "Steel bars were in short supply," Codding admitted several decades later, "so I'd lay them out while the inspectors were there, then load them behind a jeep and drag them to the next house. Finally I wore down the ends dragging them around."

By the mid-1950s, Codding Enterprises was the largest real estate firm north of San Francisco, and Santa Rosa boasted 31,000 people, having annexed Montgomery Village. Santa Rosa's expansion continued to outpace that of other cities in the county. In 1970, Santa Rosa had 48,000 people; by century's end,

Santa Rosa's precision Campion Drill Team was a highlight of local parades. Courtesy, Sonoma County Museum

the figure had jumped to 139,000 (nearly one third of the county's 445,000 total). Petaluma kept pace as the next biggest—10,300 in 1950 and 51,000 at the end of the '90s—with most of the growth east of Highway 101. Cloverdale, Sonoma, Sebastopol, Healdsburg, and Cotati remain relatively small—between 6,000 and 10,000.

With population growth came new jobs, especially when research and electronics firms discovered the area. Hewlett-Packard and Optical Coating Labs, Inc. (OCLI) brought jobs to Santa Rosa and Rohnert Park, while in the '90s electronics and computing firms began building in Petaluma.

Two cities, Rohnert Park and Windsor, grew to sudden prominence. Rohnert Park sprang up in flat farm country between Santa Rosa and Petaluma and now dwarfs neighboring Cotati. Attorneys Paul Golis and Maurice Fredericks bought Fred Rohnert's 2,700-

acre seed farm for $200 an acre in 1954. Golis served as Codding's legal adviser and then moved on to a plan of his own to create a suburb of 30,000 from scratch. He and Fredericks drew up a master plan with eight distinct neighborhood units of 250 homes each, clustered around a school and park. In 1957, Golis and Fredericks put up the first houses, and in 1962, with 2,700 residents, Rohnert Park incorporated. The city surpassed its 30,000 ceiling in the 1980s and by century's end had 40,000 people.

Rohnert Park also became the site of the North Bay's state college. Sonoma State College started life in 1956, sharing space with Santa Rosa Junior College. Guided by its first president, Dr. Ambrose Nichols, the school moved its few hundred students to the 220-acre Rohnert Park campus in 1966. By century's close, SSU (it was upgraded to a university in 1978) had 7,400 students and was granting bachelor's degrees in 37 disciplines, as well as master's degrees and teaching credentials. The campus received a major boost in the late '90s when cartoonist Charles Schulz and his wife Jean, longtime county residents, donated $5 million for a campus media center. The 215,000-square-foot Jean and Charles Schulz Information Center is scheduled to open in 2000.

In 1995, SRJC started a satellite campus on 40 acres in rapidly expanding eastern Petaluma. By the end of the decade, the Petaluma campus had nearly 6,000 students of its own, many studying business and communications, reflecting the influx of high-tech firms.

In 1950, Windsor was still a sleepy burg with 1,000 people, but in the 1980s, with lots of flat, buildable land a short drive from Santa Rosa, it exploded into a much larger city. Windsor incorporated in 1992 and attracted developers and shopping malls. By 1999, it had 20,000 people and Windsor High graduated its first senior class.

Two high schools also graduated their first class in Santa Rosa in the late 1990s, reflecting the rapid growth of Sonoma County's biggest city: Elsie Allen High, named for a celebrated Pomo leader, and Maria Carrillo High, named for the valley's first European resident.

The '60s brought waves of upheaval to Sonoma County. The Civil Rights Movement resonated in Santa Rosa in May 1962 when leaders of the local black community staged a sit-in at the Silver Dollar Cafe, which had refused to serve them. At SRJC, students launched protests of the Vietnam War, which eventually claimed the lives of over 80 locals.

In the late '60's, disaffected city dwellers dreamed of idyllic societies in rural settings, much as the utopians of Altruria and Icaria Speranza did in the late 1800s. Of all the back-to-the-land experiments, none was more controversial than Lou Gottlieb's Morning Star Ranch. Gottlieb, once a member of the Limeliters trio, bought 32 wooded acres near Graton and in 1967 invited folks from Haight-Ashbury to set up camp under the stars free of charge. An impromptu commune of huts and teepees sprang up under the trees, but county officials, citing health and safety codes, leaned on Gottlieb to break up the party and evict the campers. Gottlieb responded by deeding the property to God, prompting the county's quirkiest legal ruling: God was not eligible to own land in Sonoma County. Gottlieb reluctantly told the campers to move on; he continued to pay property taxes on God's behalf.

In the lower Russian River communities, former

During the 1986 flood along the Russian River, Guerneville residents set up their own ferry service to get to town for supplies. When the waters receded, residents rebuilt their homes—sometimes on stilts—and spruced up their resorts and businesses for upcoming summer tourist seasons. Photo by Simone Wilson

summer cabins became year-round homes. In the early '70s, grassroots newspapers like the funky Sonoma County Stump offered alternative views on county politics and commentary on the flourishing music scene. Where River resorts once resonated with sounds of the Big Band era, smaller music clubs like Garbo's, the Inn of the Beginning, and the West of the Laguna featured a home-grown folk and blues sound. Kate Wolf, who with her husband Don Coffin started the group Wildwood Flower, captured the county's people and landscape in her lyrics. She died of leukemia in 1986; an annual Kate Wolf Memorial Concert celebrates her musical vision of Sonoma County as a rural haven.

From the late '60s on, the Russian River, with its relaxed attitudes, also became a mecca for gay tourists from the Bay Area. Especially after the upscale Fife's resort opened in 1978, a festive summer scene swung into high gear, leading many gay and lesbian homeowners and business people to move into the area. That, in turn, led to a more visible presence for

SONOMA COUNTY'S A MOVIE STAR

It was *deja vu* all over again on Santa Rosa's tree-lined McDonald Avenue. On the set of *Shadow of a Doubt*, Diane Ladd, playing the naive sister of the villainous Uncle Charlie, ran up the steps of a Victorian mansion and announced his impending visit. She still sounded enthusiastic, even after 15 takes. Off camera, actor Mark Harmon, cast as the evil uncle, leaned against a tree, drinking a 1990s vintage soda pop. The film crew had returned to the scene of the crime for a *Shadow* remake for TV's Hallmark Hall of Fame.

It was *deja vu* because 50 years earlier, Alfred Hitchcock was filming just down the block. Hitchcock brought actors Joseph Cotten and Teresa Wright to Santa Rosa in 1942 because of wartime restrictions. It was the middle of World War II, and building materials for sets were in short supply. Instead of skimping on scenery for his atmospheric thriller, Hitchcock selected a real place for the idyllic small town essential to the script by Thornton Wilder.

"That's right, I want to place a call to Santa Rosa —Santa Rosa, California," Cotten tells a telephone operator at the start of the film. Cotten plays the mad, bad uncle who brings terror to his kindly relatives and their innocent town, played by Santa Rosa itself, with bit parts for the Carnegie Library, the railroad depot, the Til Two Bar and Courthouse Square. He also hired local extras, including 10-year-old Edna May Wonacott, the daughter of a Santa Rosa grocer, to play the heroine's pesky, know-it-all kid sister.

Filming the TV remake of Shadow of a Doubt on McDonald Avenue in 1991. Photo by Simone Wilson

Hitchcock chose Dr. C.M. Carlson's house on McDonald Avenue, a modest mansion with a lived-in look, for the movie family's home. "But when we came back, two weeks prior to the shooting," Hitch later recalled, "the owner was so pleased that his house was going to be in a picture that he had it completely repainted. So we had to . . . paint it dirty again." *Life* was so impressed with Hitchcock's on-location shooting the magazine ran an eight-page spread on the production in its January 25, 1943 issue.

The filmmaker was so satisfied with his Sonoma County shoot he returned 20 years later for *The Birds*, where psychotic ravens and gulls attack the inhabitants of a seaside town. Hitchcock filmed in Bodega Bay, but the coastal vistas were too pleasant for the film's gloomy tone, so footage was altered in post-production to create an eerier effect than nature provided. The mechanical birds Hitchcock ordered didn't perform well, so he brought in live birds, which consumed $1,000 worth of catered shrimp and anchovies.

Hitchcock used the Potter School in Bodega for scenes of children fleeing from a squadron of crows and shot footage at the Tides Restaurant. He also wanted a house near Bodega Bay owned by Rose Gaffney. The feisty Bay resident had just led a battle to keep PG&E from building a nuclear reactor on Bodega Head, and she was just as wary about Universal Studios. "A limousine pulled up to Rose's house," recalls Don Howe of Salmon Creek, a friend of Gaffney's. "A messenger said Mr. Hitchcock would like to speak to her. 'Who?' barked Rose. Hitchcock was taken by the fact that she didn't know him and didn't go to the movies. They later became such friends he invited her to the preview of *The Birds* in Sebastopol."

Long before Hitchcock, the county had a silent film resumé. The California Motion Picture Association shot its 1914 feature *Salomy Jane*, starring Beatrice Michelena, under the redwoods near Monte Rio. The *New York Dramatic Mirror* praised its "reel after reel of gorgeous scenes . . . with rivers breaking their way through primal forests." Michelena, the mainstay of the company, returned in 1916 for *Faust*, shot at Korbel Vineyards, and in 1925, Cecil B. DeMille brought his cameras to the Russian River for the Indian epic *Braveheart*.

Early talkies needed cumbersome sound equipment that made on-location shooting difficult. Hitchcock rediscovered Sonoma County as a movie set

A McDonald Avenue scene from Alfred Hitchcock's Shadow of a Doubt, with (left to right) Joseph Cotten, Henry Travers, Charley Bates, lSanta Rosa girl Edna May Wonacott, and Teresa Wright. Courtesy, Universal Studios

in the '40s, and movie makers have been trooping up here ever since. In 1944, *The Happy Land* marked the debut of five-year-old Natasha Gurdin (later Natalie Wood); the director spotted her while she lingered near the set, eating an ice cream cone. Cameras returned to McDonald Avenue in 1948 for Arthur Miller's World War II drama *All My Sons.* Apple ranchers and union drivers were at odds in *Thieves Highway,* a 1949 film that reflected real tensions in California agriculture. It was filmed in apple orchards near Sebastopol, and when the shoot was over, local kids made go-carts from the sets.

Santa Rosa's Carnegie Library, which had a cameo in *Shadow of a Doubt,* played a larger role in the 1956 *Storm Center,* with Bette Davis as a librarian branded as a communist for resisting censorship. Davis spent six weeks in town and picked up pointers from Ruth Hall, the town's real-life librarian.

Sonoma County's diversity is still its ticket to the movies. It provides every kind of landscape—woods, farmland, coast—and its well-preserved downtowns and neighborhoods are the perfect stand-in for New England, the rural mid-west, and Smalltown America.

Hayley Mills, then a child in pigtails, played *Pollyanna,* filmed on McDonald Avenue in 1959, and George Lucas shot parts of *American Graffiti* in Petaluma in 1972. Lassie came to Hop Kiln Winery in 1978 for *The Magic of Lassie,* and Michael Ritchie's *Smile,* 1975, lampooned Santa Rosa's beauty pageants.

Then in 1985, *Peggy Sue Got Married.* Kathleen Turner and Nicolas Cage pursued a '50s romance on the Santa Rosa High campus, inside Lena's restaurant, and on the streets of Petaluma. At the local premiere, the familiar landmarks drew more applause than the stars. The success of *Peggy Sue* caught the attention of location scouts, and from the late '80s on, dozens of movies and commercials were shot here. Francis Ford Coppola came to Sonoma in 1987 for *Tucker,* with Jeff Bridges as a maverick auto designer, and Petaluma played a '50s downtown for the 1997 remake of *Lolita.* Out in the west county, the rolling hills and coastal bluffs pose for car commercials—look for brief shots of new Fords and Mazdas zooming down rural roads with Goat Rock in the background.

MOVIES MADE IN SONOMA COUNTY

1914	Salomy Jane	1978	The Magic of Lassie
1915	Bronco Billy Anderson	1982	Shoot the Moon
1916	Faust	1984	Goonies
1926	Braveheart	1985	Peggy Sue Got
1942	Shadow of a Doubt		Married
1944	The Happy Land	1985	Howard the Duck
1944	The Fighting Sullivans	1986	Smooth Talk
1945	Captain Eddie	1988	Tucker
1947	The Farmer's Daughter	1990	Flatliners
1948	Thieves Highway	1990	Die Hard II
1948	All My Sons	1991	Shadow of a Doubt (TV)
1955	Many Rivers to Cross	1991	Stop or My Mom Will
1956	Storm Center		Shoot
1960	Pollyanna	1992	Nowhere to Run
1962	It's a Mad Mad Mad	1992	Basic Instinct
	Mad World	1995	Phenomenon
1962	The Birds	1996	Lolita
1968	Finian's Rainbow	1996	Scream
1972	The Candidate	1996	Grand Avenue (TV)
1973	American Graffiti	1996	Inventing the Abbots
1973	Steelyard Blues	1997	Paradise Cove
1975	Smile	1998	Mumford
1977	Heroes		

gays in the rest of the county, so that by 1999, the Gay and Lesbian Parade was holding its tenth annual event in Santa Rosa.

The early '60s saw the birth of a home-grown Sonoma County environmental movement. Folks in Bodega Bay are still proud of their David and Goliath encounter with Pacific Gas & Electric. In 1961, when the utility announced plans to create a nuclear power plant on Bodega Head, there was no Coastal Commission and no California Environmental Quality Act. But when the dust cleared, PG&E had scrapped its plans and there was nothing but a crater where the nuclear reactor would have been—a site locals now call "The Hole in the Head."

At first, the plans proceeded smoothly. The Public Utilities Commission gave its approval, and workers dug a 70-foot-deep shaft for the reactor. PG&E tacked up signs announcing "The Atomic Park."

Then Rose Gaffney got mad. A rancher with holdings on Bodega Head, Gaffney was (to use a geology term) flinty. Even the feisty landholder's friends called her stubborn and irascible. She had already rebuffed PG&E's attempt in the late '50s to purchase nearby Horseshoe Cove for the nuclear site. Her spread also included mud flats where fishermen moored their boats, a stretch of land PG&E now wanted to acquire for its road out to the Head. Gaffney

wasn't keen on selling and eventually got riled about the whole project. The irresistible force (the world's largest utility) had met the proverbial immovable object (Gaffney).

Locals credit the prickly rancher as the one who galvanized public opinion against the project. Other opponents included Hazel Mitchell, a Bodega Bay waitress who gathered hundreds of signatures against it, and Doris Sloan, later a professor of environmental science at UC Berkeley. When Sloan took geologist Pierre Saint-Armand on a walking tour of the site, he discovered a flaw PG&E had overlooked: the San Andreas Fault, the Bad Boy of California quakes, went right through Bodega Head. Armed with this geologic ammunition, locals lobbied against the project and the PUC canceled its permit. The dramatic 8.5 Anchorage quake in 1964 caused some slippage on Bodega Head, which put the idea to rest for good.

The scuffle over Bodega Head marked one of the first times Californians had fought against a project on environmental grounds and won. PG&E sold its bayshore land to State Parks for $1, and the Hole in the Head is now a pond, a stopover along the Pacific Flyway for ducks and herons. Horseshoe Cove is the site of the UC Davis Marine Lab, and the Head is part of Sonoma Coast State Beaches.

The next big project to stir public concern was a 5,200-acre housing project on the county's north coast. Architect Al Boeke and landscape architect Lawrence Halprin, working for the owners, Oceanic Properties, designed The Sea Ranch as an environmentally sensitive project with underground utilities, rows of redwood homes, and wide common areas sloping down to the sea. When county planners gave the two-part project the green light in 1964 and 1968, environmental interests objected to the loss of public access to ten miles of scenic coast.

County voters were asked to settle the matter in the form of Measure B. Oceanic offered 125 acres at the mouth of the Gualala River for a park, but only if voters turned thumbs down on B and public access to the Sea Ranch coast.

Petaluma veterinarian (and later county supervisor) Bill Kortum, speaking for the newly-formed COAAST (Citizens Organized to Acquire Access to State Tidelands), called the offer to donate the Gualala beach "a freshly-pulled carrot with the sand still on it." B went down to defeat, but the controversy had state-

Members of the Santa Rosa Boys Club travel through downtown Santa Rosa on the hood of a flashy DeSoto, probably for the annual spring Rose Parade. Note the old Courthouse, which was torn down in the 1970s, in the background. Courtesy, Sonoma County Museum

wide consequences. The wrangle over Sea Ranch was a major factor in the passage of the California Coastal Conservation Act of 1972 (Prop. 20). The Act created the California Coastal Commission, which now oversees building and access on California's 1,100-mile coastline. The state legislature finally resolved the access controversy, giving The Sea Ranch $500,000 in exchange for five public trails between Highway One and the shore.

The decade ended with that typical California event, a big quake—two in fact, on the evening of October 1, 1969. (One Bay Area paper called it "a shocking double feature.") Only registering 5.6 and 5.7 compared to the 7.9 rocker of 1906, the twin shake-up nevertheless seriously affected Santa Rosa's downtown. No one was killed, but the Roxy Theatre was damaged and one wall of the Miramar Bar fell into Third Street, burying two parked cars. The Montgomery Ward store on Mendocino Avenue closed for good as a result of damage and sold off its merchandise from a tent. Several landmarks were declared unsafe and demolished, including the Carnegie Library, the California Theatre (affectionately known as The Cal), and the 1910 courthouse, leaving Courthouse Square without a courthouse. South of Santa Rosa, the waters of Kawana Springs Resort, which had been staunched by earth movements during the 1906 quake, once again began to flow.

Bill and Lucy Kortum of Petaluma helped start COAAST and worked to preserve coastal access; the Kortum trail named for them winds along the bluffs between Wright's Beach and Goat Rock. Photo by Simone Wilson

The 1910 County Courthouse, built to replace the one that collapsed in the 1906 quake, was the proud centerpiece of Santa Rosa's downtown through the 1960s. Photo by Clark Nattkemper

*Cars and pedestrians on Mendocino Avenue, with the 1910 Courthouse
at the end of the street (center). Courtesy, Sonoma County Museum*

CHAPTER EIGHT

Linking Past and Present

At the threshold of a new millennium, Sonoma County finds ways to capitalize on its assets—its landscape as well as its man-made heritage such as historic town centers—preserving the past as a way of enhancing the future.

Despite rapid growth on their edges, most cities maintain their historic centers. The pride of Sonoma and Healdsburg are their classic squares lined with shops, while Sebastopol's Main Street boasts stores, cafes, and lively foot traffic. On Main and Kentucky Streets in the heart of Petaluma, shops and restaurants fill historic structures like the 1886 McNear Building and architectural gems of the early 1900s.

In the early 1980s, Santa Rosa unwisely cut its downtown center in half with the construction of a downtown mall, The Plaza. Since then, however, each half has undergone rejuvenation. Near the tracks, Old Railroad Square is an animated district with shops and restaurants. Its four stone buildings, built by stone masons from Italy around 1910, are still in use, including the railway depot restored in the '90s as a visitor's center.

On the eastern side of the mall, a renovation gave 4th Street a fresh look in the '80's, but the city lost one of its key businesses when Rosenberg's Department store closed in 1988. In 1993, after the city granted a permit to raze the store, the Sonoma County Historical Society sued to block its demolition, citing the 1937 building as a classic of *art moderne* design. Before the wrangle proceeded to the courts, a group of buyers bought the store and spruced it up for new tenants—a bookstore and coffeehouse. Today it anchors a downtown bustling with shops and sidewalk cafes.

In Sebastopol, the Western Sonoma County Historical Society restored the town's 1917 mission-style railway depot, now the West County Museum, while in Healdsburg and Petaluma, former Carnegie Libraries became spacious city museums. In the most ambitious restoration, the 1908 Santa Rosa Post Office got a slow ride to a new home. While its 5th Street neighbors were demolished to make way for the mall, several people came to the old girl's rescue, including Henry Trione, who kicked in $50,000, and Ernest Hahn, builder of the mall, with a $150,000 loan.

Under the direction of preservationist Dan Peterson, the two-story structure was hooked up to pulleys, and, in a scene reminiscent of Egyptians hauling stone blocks to the pyramids, work crews pulled the massive pile over to 7th Street. One of the best remaining examples of Classic Federal Architecture, the building was reborn in 1979 as the Sonoma County Museum.

Buildings were not the only structures people loved enough to save. When CalTrans insisted the 1922 Guerneville Bridge had to go, residents formed a grassroots committee called, variously, S.O.B. (Save Our Bridge) and the Bridge Club, and in 1989, they had it placed on the National Register. When the new concrete bridge opened in 1998, the metal bridge was set aside for walkers and cyclists. County supervisors also named 20 bridges to a Historic Bridge District in the '90s, including Wohler and Hacienda Bridges on the Russian River, and several spans over the Gualala River and Sonoma Creek.

Sonoma County boasts a vibrant arts scene, including ArtTrails, where artists open their studios to visitors twice a year, and music events like the Russian River Jazz Festival and Cotati Jazz Festival. Santa Rosa Junior College and Sonoma State University both maintain art galleries and host numerous cultural programs. Corrick Brown molded the Santa Rosa Symphony into a regional gem during his 38-year tenure as music director; in 1995, he passed the baton to Jeffrey Kahane. For film buffs, there's the Sonoma Film Institute, SSU's long-running series of foreign and classic movies.

Theatre companies like River Repertory Theatre and Actors' Theatre bring everything from Shakespeare to experimental plays to local stages. SRJC's Summer Repertory Theatre, run by Frank Zwolinski and Mollie Boice, performs a five or six-play season every summer. Founded in 1972, SRT has also become a prestigious training ground for actors and theatre technicians. Luther Burbank Center for the Arts, the county's largest performance venue, got its start in 1981 after a group of community leaders arranged to buy the complex for $4.5 million from the defunct Christian Life Center. The center hosts over a hundred events a year and also houses the California Museum of Art.

The Geysers steam fields, in the late 1800s considered a natural wonder on a par with Yosemite, were regarded as a miracle source of power in the 1950s. Courtesy, Sonoma County Museum

For two weeks in 1976, Sonoma County was at the center of the avant-garde art scene, when internationally-known Christo Javachieff set up 24 miles of white nylon curtain. The Running Fence started near Petaluma, traced a path over rolling hills, and ended with a plunge into the sea.

Annual events fill the county calendar, from Santa Rosa's Rose Parade and Windsor's Hot Air Balloon Classic to hometown celebrations like Kenwood's Fourth of July Pillow Fights and Guerneville's Stumptown Days. Capping them all is the Human Race, which began in 1982 and now draws eight to 10 thousand folks—some in costumes or body paint—who walk to raise money for a galaxy of local causes. The 1999 event raised $750,000.

Sonoma County has no national parks, but county and state have both worked to expand park holdings, not only to preserve natural features but also to highlight historic sites like Fort Ross, Jack London's ranch, and the Sonoma Mission. In 1891, Col. James Armstrong proposed selling 600 acres of redwoods at the headwaters of Fife Creek to the state for a "natural park and botanical garden." (Local timbermen noted that the Colonel was short of cash and the Grove's trees

had tested as poor for lumber anyway.) Armstrong died in 1900, but in 1917, after Guerneville ran a strong PR campaign to save the trees, county voters agreed to buy the grove for $80,000. State Parks acquired the grove in 1934 and later added to it the Austin Creek watershed.

In 1934, a caravan of autos also drove along the 10 miles of coastline between Bodega Bay and Jenner to celebrate the creation of a new state park: Sonoma Coast State Beaches. It was a good beginning for the county's coastal parks, which today encompass about two-thirds of the county's 55-mile coastline. North of the Russian River, the County Parks runs Stillwater Cove and Gualala Parks while State Parks runs Salt Point and Fort Ross. Salt Point, once the site of a busy sawmill and quarry, became a state park in 1968 and slowly expanded to encompass seven spectacular miles of rugged coast, including Gerstle Cove, one of the state's first underwater reserves.

The smallest holding in the entire State Park system is the Bufano Peace Statue acreage, a 60' by 60' bluff-top parcel topped with a mosaic-covered obelisk erected in 1969 by San Francisco artist Benny Bufano. It is also the only State Parks land whose sole brochure is a cocktail napkin: the statue's history is featured on illustrated napkins inside the adjacent Timber Cove Inn.

Fort Ross, the enclave left behind by the Russians in 1841, had just become state property when the 1906

Politicos Dan Hauser (right) and Nick Tibbets were reluctant gourmets at the annual Slugfest, an off-the-wall event celebrating the Russian River mascot, the banana slug, circa 1983. The event consisted of slug races and tastings of such unlikely dishes as slug mousse and slug a-la-king. Hauser was a state assemblyman in the 1980s and '90s. Photo by Simone Wilson

Rangers Bill Walton (left) and Dan Murley dress as a Russian officer and a Hudson Bay trader for the Living History Day at Fort Ross Historic Park, circa 1990. Photo by Simone Wilson

Benny Bufano's finished his 72-foot obelisk entitled "The Expanding Universe" on a coastal promontory in 1969. Popularly called "the Peace Statue," it stands on state park land near Timber Cove Inn. Photo by Simone Wilson

quake toppled the chapel and damaged the Fort. Over the years, State Parks worked to recreate it as it looked in the 1830s, rebuilding the stockade, barracks, commandant's house, and chapel. Every July, rangers and members of the Fort Ross Interpretive Association stage a Living History Day, recreating a day in 1836, when Mexican officers from Sonoma show up and invite the Russians to go home. The Russians politely refuse, fire off their muskets as a show of strength, and invite the Mexicans to stay and party.

Annadel was once the private reserve of Joe Coney, a latter-day merchant prince who bought the land in the 1930s. Coney owned steamship companies, cattle ranches, and several thousand acres east of Santa Rosa, where he hosted scout encampments and military maneuvers. He also created Lake Ilsanjo—named for himself and his wife Ilsa. Financial setbacks in the '60s prompted him to sell the acreage; some went for development, including Oakmont. The remainder was up for sale when tycoon Henry Trione plunked down $450,000 to reserve most of it for a park. Annadel's 5,000 acres of oak woodland became a state park in 1971.

Residents have also worked to preserve landscape and natural resources, whether as parks or as commercial enterprises. In the 1920s, utility companies harnessed the Geysers, tapping fissures in the volcanic

Kenwood Depot, once a stop on the rail line between Sonoma and Santa Rosa, has been restored for use as a community hall. Courtesy, Sonoma County Museum

Mayacamas hills. The initial scheme failed when steam corroded the 1920s vintage turbines. In the '50s, engineers took another look to see whether, as the *Press Democrat* put it, the Geysers were "a useless freak of nature or cheap, limitless power." Those tests hailed geothermal energy as the miracle power source of the future. By 1973, private companies had drilled over 100 wells and the steam fields were the biggest geothermal energy resource in the world. In the 1980s, prices slumped and the subterranean steam itself was being depleted. In the late 1990s, Santa Rosa city engineers proposed piping the city's treated effluent to the Geysers to replenish the steam fields; the project was in the works as the century drew to a close.

If agriculture continues to flourish, it will be due to the wine industry, with its high cash-per-acre yields. With 45,000 acres of vineyards in the county, grapes are the most visible and lucrative of Sonoma's products. Wineries not only preserve the region's rural character but also draw tourists, another vital component of the local economy.

Although some Sonoma County wineries survived Prohibition, its repeal did not bring a wine Renaissance, and in the 1950s, only 20 wineries remained. But in the late '60s, entrepreneurs began reviving wineries and experimenting with new technology. In the Russian River, Dry Creek, and Sonoma Valleys, they started new wineries or resurrected old ones, tinkering with new varietals and replacing wood vats with gleam-

Children play in the sun at Goat Rock near Jenner, part of Sonoma Coast State Beaches. Photo by Simone Wilson

ing stainless steel. And they began winning coveted awards, proving quality local wines could rival pricey European ones.

In the 1970s, when Americans began discovering international cuisine and fine wines, Sonoma County vintners were ready for them. Suddenly winemaking was a multi-million dollar business that attracted rich, out-of-state investors. Schlitz Brewing purchased Geyser Peak in the 1970s, and in the '90s wineries were still changing hands: French conglomerate Moet-Hennessey/Louis Vuitton bought Simi Winery, founded by San Francisco wine dealers Giuseppe and Pietro Simi in 1876. Sonoma-Cutrer, founded in 1973, sold its winery and chardonnay vines in 1999 to Kentucky conglomerate Brown-Forman Corp.

Other wineries continue under family direction. Gundlach-Bundschu, founded in 1858, closed during Prohibition but was reborn in 1973 and is still run by great-great-great grandsons of co-founder Jacob Gundlach. Samuele Sebastiani came to Sonoma from

Tuscany at the turn of the century. Today his grandson Don Sebastiani owns Sebastiani Winery, while Don's brother Sam founded Viansa Winery south of town.

Sonoma County faces the challenge of maintaining ecological diversity amid the wine industry's phenomenal success. Prices of vineyard land doubled in the last five years of the century, and in 1999, was going for as much as $58,000 per acre with established vines. As a result, corporations like Gallo are increasingly buying up land and introducing agribusiness where small holdings and oak woodland had been before.

As prices of vineyard land increased, apple orchards were pulled up and planted in grapes. Gravenstein apples remain the pride of Sebastopol, but only 4,000 acres of apple orchard remained at the end

Sonoma County Museum today. Inset: Santa Rosa's 1910 post office hitches a ride to its new job as the Sonoma County Museum. Courtesy, Sonoma County Museum

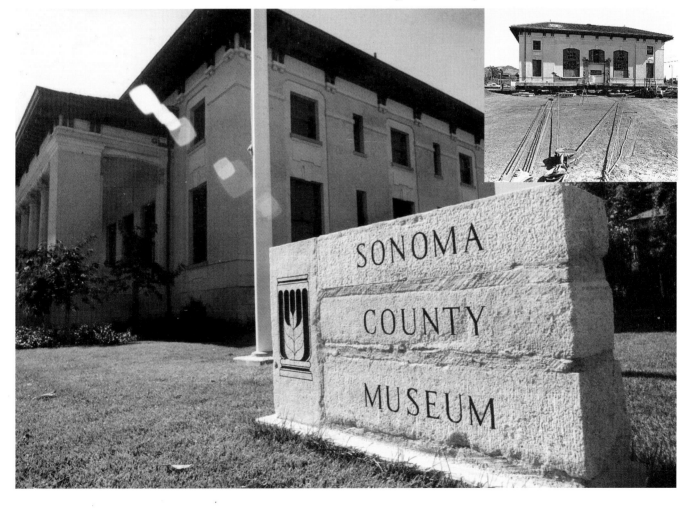

WRITERS AND ARTISTS OF SONOMA COUNTY

CHARLES SCHULZ created the Peanuts comic strip in 1950 and has lived in Sonoma County since 1958. He also owns the Redwood Empire Ice Arena, where a real zamboni grooms the ice. In the late 1990s, he and his wife Jean donated $5 million to Sonoma State University for a media center.

M.F.K. (MARY FRANCES KENNEDY) FISHER, for 50 years one of America's premier food writers, was the author of *How to Cook a Wolf, Gastronomical Me* and 20 other books on food, culture and a philosophy of living well—works that made her the doyenne of an American food Renaissance in the '70s and '80s. A southern California native, in 1970 she moved to Glen Ellen, where a sign by her front door read: "Friends—ring bell and come in. Foes—enter any old way." She died in 1992.

OTTO HAGEL AND HANSEL MIETH-HAGEL were childhood friends in Germany. As teenagers, with Hansel disguised as Otto's little brother, they took to

Hansel Mieth-Hagel and dogs at the Geysers, 1958. Photo by Otto Hagel, courtesy Sonoma County Museum

Charles M. Schulz, creator of Charlie Brown, Linus, Lucy, Snoopy, and the rest of the Peanuts gang, was born in 1922 in Minneapolis, Minnesota, where he grew up playing ice hockey and sketching in the classroom. He brought his family to Sonoma County in 1958, where he continued playing ice hockey and sketching. Courtesy, United Media, a Scripps Howard Company

the road, photographing people in neighboring countries. In the early 1930s, they immigrated to America and photographed migrants during the Depression, selling their work for enough cash to refill their gas tank. Mieth was the second woman photographer hired by *Life* magazine (Margaret Bourke-White was the first) and was on the magazine's staff from 1937 to 1950. In 1941, they bought a rural retreat in the hills west of Santa Rosa, drawn to Sonoma County by Jack London's stories. Blacklisted as leftists during the

The interior of Luther Burbank's glass and metal greenhouse, which miraculously survived the 1906 quake. Burbank was more an observer than a theoretician, but he wrote extensively about his plant experiments, issued annual catalogues of "New Creations," and carried on a correspondence with luminaries of his day such as Edison, Ford and John Muir. The greenhouse is on the grounds of the Luther Burbank Home in Santa Rosa. Photo by Simone Wilson

Benny Bufano's statue "Shadows of the Future" in the courtyard of the Sonoma County Library in downtown Santa Rosa. Bufano's sculptures of people and animals emphasized streamlined shapes and elegant lines. The obelisk at Timber Cove is another Bufano work. Photo by Simone Wilson

McCarthy era, they retreated to the ranch but continued to photograph Sonoma County's people and landmarks. Otto died in 1973, Hansel in 1998 at the age of 88.

Internationally known potter MARGUERITE WILDENHAIN studied at Germany's Bauhaus School, the nexus of the modern art movement. She fled Germany in 1938 and came to Sonoma County in 1941 in hopes of starting a new Bauhaus center. With friends,

Muralist Emil Zakheim worked with Diego Rivera and painted some of the murals inside Coit Tower. Courtesy, Sonoma County Museum

she founded Pond Farm on the grounds of Armstrong Woods State Preserve near Guerneville. Students from around the world came to her summer pottery seminars, making Sonoma County a mecca for students of modern art in the 1940s and '50s. The school disbanded in the 1950s, but Wildenhain continued to live and teach at Pond Farm until 1979. She died there in 1985 at the age of 88.

BERNARD ZAKHEIM studied with Diego Rivera and in the 1930s was one of the 26 muralists who painted the frescoes inside San Francisco's Coit Tower. He also painted the extensive murals at the medical school of the University of California and sold some of his 350 paintings to the San Francisco Museum of Art. In 1941, he moved to Sebastopol and turned his attention to wood sculpture; much of his work was a protest against injustice, including Nazi repression and suppression of artistic freedom in the Soviet Union.

CAROLYN KIZER's *Yin* won the Pulitzer Prize for Poetry in 1985. She taught at Stanford and Princeton and in the late '60s was the first director of the literature program for the National Endowment for the Arts. Kizer and her husband, architect John Woodbridge, moved to Sonoma in 1988.

of the '90s. In 1999, the Hallberg family, in the apple business since the 1880s, sold its ranch to Sonoma-Cutrer. Another major blow came in 1999 with the closure of Sebastopol's Vacu-dry, the nation's second largest apple drying plant and chief buyer for local apple growers.

Hops, which died out as a Sonoma County crop in the '50s, regained a foothold in 1996 when Benziger Family Winery tore up several acres of merlot and planted hops for its crafted brews. The enthusiasm for hops corresponds with the phenomenal rise in microbreweries. Grace Brother's Acme Beer made a brief comeback in 1986 when businessman Peter Eierman's Xselsior Brewery revived the Acme label. By century's end, California had 90 microbreweries, including Bear Republic Brewing in Healdsburg, Powerhouse Brewing in Sebastopol, and Dempsey's in Petaluma.

In both Sonoma and Napa, winemaking dovetailed with a tourism boom. In the mid-1970s gasoline prices skyrocketed, and Bay Area vacationers, instead of zooming off to Lake Tahoe, switched to destinations an hour's drive away like the Russian River, redwoods, and Sonoma Coast. Wineries in the northern part of the county, organized by wine publicist Millie Howie, banded together in 1974 to form the Russian River Wine Road, a self-guiding tour of wineries in the Russian River watershed. Nine wineries pooled resources and printed a map to lure tourists away from Napa and up Highway 101. The Wine Road held its 20th annual Barrel Tasting in 1999, and its 65-plus members draw tourists whose dollars support restaurants, bed and breakfast inns, stores, and the wineries themselves.

Agriculture is not only a mainstay of the county's prosperity but an avenue for waves of immigrants. Just as Italians and Japanese came over a century ago and first labored on the land, in the past decades, workers from Mexico migrated here and are now about 10 percent of the population. In the '80s and '90s, immigrants from Cambodia and Eritrea added to the county's cultural mix.

The Pomo and Coast Miwok, the first people of Sonoma County, are still a visible presence and a reminder that all other immigrants are relative newcomers. Isabel Kelly, the UC Berkeley doctoral student who did extensive anthropological field work on the Coast Miwok in the 1930s, was convinced the two elderly Miwok she interviewed were the last of their tribe. In Kelly's time, prejudice against Native Americans may have made them reluctant to come forward. Far from being obliterated, in 1992 Coast Miwoks formed a tribal government under the name Federated Coast Miwok and are working to achieve federal tribal status and regain rights to their rancheria in Graton. In Marin, MAPOM (Miwok Archaeological Preserve of Marin) maintains a museum of Miwok culture, holds classes in traditional arts, grants scholarships to Miwok students, and publishes books by and about tribe members. MAPOM also works in concert with Point Reyes National Seashore, where Kule Loklo, a recreated Miwok village, is a site for classes and festivals.

Pomos, who reside in Sonoma, Mendocino, and Lake Counties, work with local museums to display their superb basketry as a

Rosenberg's Department Store (on Fourth St. looking west towards D St.) circa 1940s. The store closed in 1988 and the building, a classic of art moderne *architecture, was saved from demolition. Courtesy, Sonoma County Museum*

The NWP train (coming from the right) crosses the Hacienda Bridge over the Russian River, 1908. The bridge was converted to auto traffic in the 1930s, but otherwise looks the same today as it did in earlier days. Bert Travis collection.

St. Teresa's Church, which is still in use, is one of the gems of the town of Bodega. Photo by Simone Wilson

way of teaching about their ongoing culture. Both Grace Hudson Museum in Ukiah and Jesse Peter Museum at SRJC serve as outlets for communicating Pomo culture to others. In the '90s, an exhibition at the Grace Hudson Museum (later shown at the Oakland Museum), "Remember Your Relations: The Elsie Allen Baskets, Family and Friends," revealed the importance—both practical and ceremonial—of baskets in the lives of those who made and used them. Although most baskets either wore out or were ceremonially destroyed when the weaver died, Annie Burke (1876-1962), a weaver and teacher, asked her daughter, Elsie Allen, not to destroy her baskets but to preserve them to educate others. Allen added to the collection and passed it on to her eldest daughter, Genevieve Allen Aguilar. This remarkable assembly of over 130 baskets includes information most collections lack: information about the artists and about the baskets as a focus of Pomo culture. Elsie Allen died in 1990; Santa Rosa named a new high school after her.

In 1999, the Smithsonian Institution sponsored workshops on Pomo culture, including one in front of Warm Springs Dam. Built in 1983, the dam flooded sedge beds where the Dry Creek Pomo traditionally collected material for baskets. The event celebrated the creation of new sedge beds so that Pomo artistry, the first ever practiced in Sonoma County, would continue as one of the many cultural threads that make up the life of Sonoma County.

Cleveland and Schurman's hay and grain business on Third Street in Santa Rosa was the backdrop for a staff shot of Red Wagon Delivery Service's drivers and trucks in 1921. Santa Rosa's livery stables were regular customers for Cleveland and Schurman, but trucks like the ones parked here signaled the end of horses in commerce. Courtesy, Sonoma County Library

Chronicles of Leadership

Since the days of the California gold rush, Sonoma County's hospitable climate and fertile soil have lured many settlers filled with hopes and dreams. Various types of businesses, many directly tied to the land, have thrived throughout the county.

The foothills and slopes along the eastern part of the county have been draped with vineyards since Mexican General Mariano Vallejo established the first commercial winegrowing operation in the 1850s. Mission grape stock brought to California by the early Spanish Franciscan padres provided the fruit from which Vallejo made his wine. By the mid-1850s Hungarian nobleman Agostin Haraszthy, a viticulturist who imported top-quality grape cuttings from Europe, significantly improved the quality of wine produced in eastern Sonoma County. Wine making has become Sonoma County's number one industry.

South of the vineyard-covered hills, Sonoma County flattens out into fertile flatland that stretches from east to west across the entire width of the county to the Pacific Ocean. From gold rush days to the present day, all types of livestock have grazed on the fertile, flat fields.

Water transportation along the Petaluma and Sonoma rivers, San Pablo Bay, and the Pacific Ocean permitted meat and produce to be shipped to markets in the Bay Area. During the late nineteenth century, ice cars did much to encourage growth of dairies in southern Sonoma County.

Vast stands of redwoods still cover the northern and western regions of the county. During the years of Mexican rule, Anglo settlers in western Sonoma County manufactured lumber using pit saws. By the 1850s commercial logging operations were established. The number of mills and amount of lumber produced grew rapidly during the following half-century. As redwoods in easily accessible areas became scarce, improvements in technology enabled loggers to reach deeper into more remote areas to harvest timber.

The western edge of Sonoma County snuggles up to the mighty Pacific Ocean. After serving as a route by which goods were shipped into and sent from the county for more than 100 years, the ocean now serves as a place where tourists come in search of solitude and escape from city life. The beauty of Sonoma County's rugged coastline and expansive beaches provide inspiration for writers and artists and regeneration for a growing number of people each year.

The businesses and organizations whose histories appear on the following pages have chosen to support this important literary and civic event. They illustrate the variety of ways in which individuals and their businesses have contributed to the county's growth and development. The civic involvement of Sonoma County's businesses, institutions of learning, and local government, in cooperation with its citizens, has made the area an exceptional place in which to live and work.

BALLETTO RANCH INC.

John Balletto founded Balletto Ranch, Inc. in 1977 as a sole proprietorship, at the age of 17. His father had just passed away from cancer and John needed a way to provide for himself and his mother. His parents owned five acres of land in southern Sebastopol, on which his father had farmed a couple acres of zucchini as a hobby. It had always been his father's dream to farm again, just as his Italian immigrant family had done in the Colma and Daly City areas of San Francisco, long before the development of those cities.

Out of necessity, John chose to forgo college and what looked like a promising football career to stay home and start a farming business. With his mother's kitchen table as his first office and he and his mom the first employees, John began a company, now known as Balletto Ranch, Inc. That first year John sold his zucchini on consignment to San Francisco produce houses for 50 cents per 28-pound carton. Minimum wage back then was $3.30 per hour.

As the farm's reputation for quality fresh packed zucchini grew, so did the orders. In 1977, Safeway Stores became interested in the squash Balletto Ranch was producing. In 1981, John purchased his first ranch with the help of Pete Barbieri, an Analy High School counselor and real estate agent that had taken John under his wing after the passing of John's father. The ranch was 40 acres of land located on Guerneville Road. This became the new Balletto Ranch headquarters, with a packing shed, a cooler and an office. Nineteen eighty-three saw the first crop disaster, with a disease common to squash called mosaic virus. When the virus wiped out the entire squash crop, John decided that diversification was key to staying in business. He began

planting other produce such as lettuces, greens (mustard, collards, kale, etc.) and beets. Again, business grew, and Balletto Ranch leased more property. The next challenge he faced was overcoming a major flood in 1984, which destroyed the entire winter crop.

John married Teresa Cain of Penngrove in 1988. Together, along with their employees, they grew the ranch to over 700 acres of land—the largest produce farming operation north of the Golden Gate Bridge. Produce brands included: Mama Balletto squash (after John's mother), Jacqueline gourmet salad (after their first-born daughter) and Caterina lettuce and greens (after their second daughter).

With the cost of leasing land rising, the Ballettos decided to purchase 280 acres of land on Occidental Road along the Laguna de Santa Rosa. There they built a new state-of-the-art warehouse and packing facility, along with new offices. The farm survived even

though there were more floods in 1995, 1996 and 1997.

Nineteen ninety-eight was another challenging year, with the "El Nino" rains lasting until June 24th—a time by which they should have already been well into the first squash harvest. Prices were down due to competition from Mexico, and there were negotiations for the first United Farm Workers (UFW) contract in Sonoma County in many years. The officers of the newly-formed corporation Balletto Ranch Inc. decided it was time to diversify even more. They agreed that the property on Occidental Road was much more valuable producing grapes than vegetables. The first planting of Chardonnay grapes happened in June 1999. The family at Balletto Ranch looks forward to its first vintage of Laguna Oaks premium Chardonnay.

Jacqueline and Caterina Balleto, daughters of John and Terri Balletto.

CARLILE • MACY

Carlile • Macy was formed in 1996 as a merger of two firms which both trace their history back for nearly half a century. While witnessing the growth of Santa Rosa from a small town to the regional economic center it is today, the firm takes pride in having provided designs for much of the public infrastructure serving the com-munity, as well as for many residential and commercial projects which provide housing, jobs and services to the people of Sonoma County.

Civil engineering and land surveying services have been, and continue to be, the primary focus of the firm. In the early days, plans and maps were hand-drawn with ink pen, on either vellum tracing paper or specially-treated linen cloth. Calculations were done by hand, or a slide rule or rotary calculator aided by thick mathematics tables was utilized. Surveying measurements were made with an optical transit and steel tape.

Today, the modern surveyor is equipped with a total station which measures both angle and distance, inputting data directly to the computer. Global positioning satellite systems establish primary survey control, and topographic mapping of the ground is prepared from aerial photo-grammetry. In the office, engineers and surveyors perform all of their calculations utilizing high-speed computers and specifically-designed software

This 1890 historic structure has been renovated as "The Engineers Design Depot."

The interior space provides modern design tools in a creative atmosphere.

programs. The draftsman of yesteryear has given way to highly-trained technicians who prepare plans and maps on computer-based systems which automatically plot the completed drawings in a matter of seconds.

The firm has been involved in the design of the urban, suburban, and rural fabric of Sonoma County through a constantly changing evolution. From the small cottage housing of the '50s and the suburban sprawl of the '60s and '70s, to the planned unit developments of the '70s and '80s, development patterns have now returned in the '90s to traditional neighborhood designs. Rather than the widespread developments of the past which were limited only by market forces, today planners have urban growth boundaries, building permit allocations, and public services which are stretched to their capacity.

Carlile • Macy now provides urban planning and landscape architecture to its clients to deal with the intricate designs of in-fill projects and urban redevelopment. The focus of designs is now to provide alternatives to the automobile by making neighborhoods pedestrian friendly, narrowing streets to calm traffic, adding bicycle paths, and providing opportunities for public transit. The cities of Sonoma County are rediscovering their down-

town areas and returning them to the vibrant centers of commerce and entertainment they once enjoyed. Carlile • Macy has the staff and experience to assist these communities in attaining their dreams.

The successful merger of Carlile • Macy now includes a staff of 50, which positions the firm to meet the needs of its public and private clients into the 20th century. The principals recently purchased a former railroad warehouse, in historic Railroad Square, which was originally constructed in 1890 and was one of only a few masonry buildings to survive the 1906 earthquake. This proud structure has been completely renovated as the Engineer's Design Depot, to provide a creative office environment.

Each of the firm's principals have been practicing civil engineering in Sonoma County for more than 30 years. In addition to the many projects influenced by their designs, they have left their mark on the community by a long history of public involvement. From professional organizations to business associations, non-profit boards to city commissions and boards, they have given, and continue to give, back to the community.

As Sonoma County moves into the 21st century, Carlile • Macy has the resources and talented staff to partner with its clients in providing successful projects that are assets to the community.

HUGH B. CODDING

Hugh B. Codding began as a home builder in 1939 at the age of 21. He received his general contractors license in California after serving a three-year apprenticeship as a carpenter, fresh out of high school.

Hugh Codding had built 43 houses in Santa Rosa, California by December 7, 1941. The day after Pearl Harbor, Hugh enlisted in the Sea Bees 48th U.S. Naval Construction Battalion, "for the duration." Hugh spent three years in the Pacific, building air fields and supporting facilities in the island-hopping campaign that finally led to victory. There he came face to face with challenges threatening the construction business, including malaria, heat, material shortages and snafus in the chain of command—not to mention enemy action and extremely tight time schedules.

Discharged from the Navy after the war with $400 in his pocket, Hugh Codding took up his civilian building career once again. In 1947, he founded the company that was to become the present Codding Enterprises, and built some 3,000 houses in Santa Rosa during the post-war years. The challenges faced and overcome by the Sea Bees in the Pacific stood Hugh in good stead in Santa Rosa. This time, the challenges included lack of financing caused by cycles of tight money, fluctuating interest rates, and fluctuating costs of lumber and other building materials. As with the Sea Bees and the Pacific air bases, the houses in Santa Rosa had to be completed on schedule, as the costs of construction borrowing and overhead could be devastating to a business. Many of Hugh's competitors fell by the wayside during these years and wound up in bankruptcy—a specter that

Hugh Codding became a major builder in Sonoma County after World War II.

faced Codding at least once, but was narrowly avoided.

Realizing that the new residents of the houses he was building would require places to shop, Codding built his first shopping center, Town and Country, in Santa Rosa in 1947. Codding sold that center, at a profit, but became increasingly interested in commercial development and management. Commercial centers, where the ownership and management was retained, would result in a steady rental income

stream which would be less impacted by downturns in the housing market, tight money, or other adverse factors in the pure construction business. Thus, in 1950, Codding built a major shopping center called Montgomery Village, containing more than 100 stores. Montgomery Village, 50 years later, is still one of the most successful shopping centers in Northern California.

With his flair for publicity, Codding made a name for himself during the development of Montgomery Village, on both the local and national levels. Publicity stunts such as building a house in three hours and nine minutes and a church in five hours and 16 minutes earned him recognition from Time Magazine and other national publications, as the personification of the post-WWII construction boom.

The rapid development of the Montgomery Village Shopping Center and its surrounding neighborhoods—all built by Codding—prompted the City of Santa Rosa to pursue annexation, a move which would nearly double Santa Rosa's population overnight. Codding resisted, threatening instead to incorporate Montgomery Village into it's own city. After a five-year battle between Codding and the City of Santa Rosa, Codding finally agreed to annexation in 1955 in return for certain concessions from the City. As a result, Santa

Church built by Codding Construction in just five hours, 16 minutes, in Santa Rosa, California.

Rosa's population jumped from 18,000 to 30,000 with the stroke of a pen.

Codding Enterprises continued its commercial activities in the 1960s by building the Coddingtown

House built by Codding Construction in only three hours, 9 minutes, in Santa Rosa, California.

Regional Mall in Santa Rosa, which currently houses Macy's, J.C. Penney, and Gottschalks as its major tenants. This enclosed mall has some 120 additional retail tenants, and is one of the major retail centers between San Francisco and Portland, Oregon. Codding Enterprises retains 100% ownership and management of Coddingtown.

Changing customer habits in the 1980s and recessionary times in the '90s have dictated a change in strategy for Codding Enterprises. Anticipating the retail trend toward discount outlets, Codding Enterprises has developed a "power center" in Rohnert Park, California, containing Burlington Coat Factory, Target, Wal Mart and Home Depot as its major anchors.

Codding Enterprises today owns and manages nine shopping centers including Coddingtown and Montgomery Village, and numerous other free-standing commercial buildings, apartments, motels and industrial/warehouse facilities. All but one of these properties, Merced Mall in Merced, California, is located in Sonoma County.

The success of the company has allowed Hugh Codding, along with his wife Connie, to be generous philanthropists, through the Codding Foundation, a non-profit organization established for the sole purpose of contributing to the community of Sonoma County. In addition to the efforts of the Codding Foundation, Codding has often donated his Codding Construction Company toward the building of facilities to various volunteer organizations, focusing on those designed for the well-being of Sonoma County's youth and the indigent.

CROSSCHECK, INC.

In the early 1980s, two men—one in California and one in Florida—began a quest for the same vision. Working at first individually, they both shared a desire to make a monumental change in the way financial services would be sold and delivered to the marketplace. Together they saw the possibility of changing an industry. What started out on separate coasts as separate companies was to become, in just a few short years, a major financial service company headquartered in Sonoma County.

These two men were Timothy LaBadie and Paul Green. Timothy and Paul had each already had a measure of success in business; Timothy built a retail music business as well as music production company and Paul, as the president of a highly successful, publicly-traded financial service company. They looked at business as artists would; they loved the process, the challenge and creativity of building a company and providing the leadership to change the focus

CrossCheck CEO, Paul Green.

Art is an integral part of the corporate environment at CrossCheck which mixes antique prints with modern originals.

and direction of the industry. On the West Coast, Timothy had researched leading check service providers and was convinced that services could be offered more cost-effectively than those provided by the large, national companies. His goals included a sales force with national reach and presence. He had an eye for innovation and technology, and little tolerance for stale business practices.

On the East Coast, Paul was changing the way bankcard services were sold. Through an innovative marketing approach, Paul first convinced some small banks and later, Citicorp Bank, to allow non-bank employees to sell bankcard services, for the first time ever. They established an early relationship with Citicorp that allowed them to represent Citicorp's bankcard program to merchants throughout the United States. Paul, through his company, Unlimited Marketing Service Association, and later American Marketing Corporation (AMCOR) was rewriting the rules of marketing and the cost of bankcard sales on a national level.

Sharing experience and vision, Timothy and Paul knew that they could create a strong business organization that addressed the challenges of the financial service marketplace and would benefit business and consumer alike. This vision would bring an electronic authorization terminal to more than 6 million businesses and

reduce the cost of accepting bankcards to all retailers. It would also create a national, low-cost sales channel by sharing the cost of each sale across multiple products and services, some of which would be proprietary services. Out of this vision grew a national sales channel of Independent Sales Professionals, which would come to be known as ISOs.

Paul, originally from California, moved west with his family, and he and Timothy pooled their efforts in late 1984 to help each other bring the vision to life. CrossCheck and its satellite companies were born. They opened a small office in Petaluma, and their success came from their ability to communicate this vision to an elite group of highly-motivated employees who were given the freedom to be different in approach and method. From the beginning, all the employee focus was on form rather than substance, reasoning that it was not the individual business decision that was important, but rather how each decision is made. If the decision method was sound, the overall business would be sound, replicable and eventually, profitable. But, most of all it had to be fun.

In addition to its bankcard services, CrossCheck was the first national company to offer check approval and point-of-sale. The results were phenomenal. In its first year of business, CrossCheck and its bankcard arm, AMCOR, achieved $1.3 billion in annual bank merchant processing; both the equipment and check service company began to take shape.

A large part of this early success came from marketing services through ISOs, which became thousands of "feet on the street." This was the beginning of a new industry. These independent sales

The gifted painter, Alexandra Nechita, was twelve years old when she created this striking piece.

representatives marketed bankcard services, point-of-sale equipment, check services and debit card and American Express, and were paid a lifetime residual. CrossCheck still pays bankcard and check rebates to their original ISOs, many of whom are millionaires today. The bank processing world was changing at this time from paper-based—a very expensive system—to electronic. Today, bankcard transactions are virtually all processed electronically, and it is the ISO that can be credited with this efficient change, and the vision that created the sales channel process.

As the number of ISOs increased

and more of these organizations became competitive to CrossCheck and AMCOR, Paul saw the need to create a communications vehicle to address this unique industry. Through a newsletter, *The Green Sheet,* Paul reported industry news, sales tips, marketing research and new product information. Today, this business has become a full-scale publishing business, and the newsletter has also given birth to a magazine and books on selling and banking technology. These publications are read by thousands of ISOs, mid-scale banks as well as community banks, financial service companies and equipment manufacturers and are a renowned source of financial research.

In the 1990s, to compliment the ISO sales force, Timothy and Paul added a field sales division and telesales and telemarketing groups. This gave the company the ability to focus on specific target markets, and the ability to create national sales leads for field employees, ISOs and other business partners. The emphasis on sales led to annual company growth of over 40% per year. Due to this remarkable growth, CrossCheck was experiencing an increasing need for skilled and motivated employees. Expanding their workforce across the nation was not as challenging as filling open positions in Sonoma

County. As luck would have it, Sonoma County was growing at a rapid pace at the same time, and many talented individuals moved into the region and became interested in the vision.

Since the beginning, Timothy and Paul's unique business philosophy was reflected in the work environment. Employees are heavily challenged, pushed and allowed to grow. Before many other companies realized the value of a flexible, creative workplace, CrossCheck was allowing their employees the freedom of a casual dress atmosphere and choice of benefit plans. Training and workshops foster personal and professional growth. The founders' love of art is expressed throughout the offices and makes a colorful and productive atmosphere. The quality art collection of over 70 pieces includes works on display by Pablo Picasso, John Lennon, Peter Max, and Salvador Dali. Timothy and Paul even include a few of their own pieces. Art tours are held regularly for the enjoyment of corporate visitors and staff.

To sustain the momentum that CrossCheck has had from the outset, Timothy and Paul embraced technologies in payment processing and communications that would encourage and nurture growth for years to come. By developing an alternate communications approach to the standardized IBM series 1 and further creating communications interconnectivity between a home-grown phone switch and an IBM AS400, a high speed, low cost, point-of-sale authorization solution as well as an automated dial system broke new ground in terms of both traditional capabilities and design. CrossCheck has become a recognized leader in the technology of its business and has designed hardware and software systems that address

Street art is represented by these three pieces done by graffiti-inspired artists.

the evolving financial service industry. An additional company—Concepts Inc.—was formed as part of the CrossCheck family of businesses to create and patent products for use worldwide.

In 1997, a commitment to product planning and development led the company to realize the need for an e-commerce payment solution to serve customers not able or willing to use credit cards online. The first and only web-based check writer programs on the Internet—ChecksByNet and CheckNow—were introduced. With these patent-pending programs, online customers were able to visit a web-store and pay by check. CrossCheck's technology enabled an Internet merchant to accept a check at their virtual store and print out a check ready for bank deposit at their business location seconds later. This revolutionary technology is in use by thousands of online merchants providing goods and services to Internet users.

Now, as CrossCheck readies to enter the next millennium, the company inhabits a large office park in Rohnert Park, employing over 275 Sonoma County residents and

thousands of representatives nationwide, including at a second data center in Wisconsin. CrossCheck is the largest, independently-owned payment guarantee company in the country. It presently provides payment approval and Internet services and transaction processing to tens of thousands of merchants throughout the U.S., and reports financial news and income opportunities through its publishing business, both in print and online.

CrossCheck has positioned itself to remain an industry leader well into the 21st century. With the move towards e-commerce, globalization, and the electronification of the check, CrossCheck will be the provider for transaction processing for both physical and virtual payment transactions. This direction combines the innovative spirit with the experience and knowledge necessary to take financial services to the next level. Much the way an artist looks to the sky for inspiration, Timothy and Paul look toward the future and find inspiration and excitement in the unknown.

DRY CREEK VINEYARD

Sailing ships and a dry creek seem odd partners, but for the family-owned Dry Creek Vineyard, they fit together perfectly.

To begin with, making great wines and sailing are passions of Vineyard founder and president, Dave Stare—passions which are both driven by a desire for excellence. Moreover, both embody romance and freedom of spirit, qualities which set Dry Creek Vineyard apart from other vineyards, and which make great ships an ideal symbol for its award-winning wines.

Stare founded Dry Creek Vineyard in 1972, after taking graduate courses in enology and viticulture at the University of California. It was the first new winery in Dry Creek Valley since the days of Prohibition. A city boy from Boston and previously an industrial engineer, Stare sailed against conventional wisdom, planting new grape vines in an area which had seen dozens of wineries close their doors. When he began, there were only three producers in the Valley; a quarter of a century later, more than two-dozen flourished.

Drawing on wisdom gathered during travels in France and Germany, Stare planted varieties traditionally considered inappropriate for the Valley—and proved local lore incorrect. He quickly became an industry leader and, in the years that followed served as president of the Society of Blancs, the Winegrowers of Dry Creek Valley, and the Sonoma County Wineries Association.

In 1986, after she graduated from San Francisco State University, Dave's daughter Kim, joined the Vineyard as vice president and director of marketing. Kim's husband, Don Wallace, took charge of day-to-day vineyard and winery operations. The family surrounded itself with other experienced, dedicated and committed staff, many of whom were with the Stares for more than two decades, as the millennium drew toward its close.

Grapes from Dry Creek Vineyard's 1972 vintage were the first—and last—to be crushed away from the estate. Its original 3,500-square-foot winery was built in 1973, and all subsequent vintages were made on the estate.

From the beginning, making wine was a personal operation. Grapes from each of the estate's vineyards—Sauvignon Blanc, Cabernet, Chardonnay, Merlot, Zinfandel grapes and others—were crushed and fermented separately, as were lots purchased from other vineyards throughout the region. Many of these were sources of Dry Creek grapes for decades, and were intimately understood by Dry Creek's wine-making staff.

As each lot aged, there were from 70 to 100 individual component wines from each vintage that Stare and his staff tasted, using their expertise to decide which to blend. They also identified those rare vintages that are truly extraordinary, and used them to make outstanding reserve wines. Production was always done to taste, not to some blind formula, and the title "reserve" went only to superlative wines, not just to improve sales.

Dry Creek scored numerous firsts—both in wine competitions and broader arenas. It produced the first Fume Blanc from Dry Creek Valley, introduced Bordeaux blending, and originated—and obtained in 1983 legal recognition for—the Dry

David Stare founded his Sonoma County winery in 1972. His love of the sea is reflected in the spirited paintings which grace each bottle of wine from Dry Creek Vineyard.

Creek Valley regional appellation. Passionate about wine and its customers, driving for perfection and committed to innovation, Dry Creek Vineyard has established its branding without becoming complacent. Family ownership allows it to be proactive, experimenting with new vineyards, new techniques and new varietals, such as a Zinfandel Grappa introduced in 1998.

As to the sailboats, they first appeared in 1982 on Dry Creek's labels which, in the year's that followed, showcased dozens of specially commissioned paintings commemorating the romance of the sea and of the vine.

Dry Creek Vineyard is located in the heart of Sonoma County's Dry Creek Valley. Founded in 1972, the ivy-covered stone winery is reminiscent of country chateau-style french architecture.

EYE ASSOCIATES OF SEBASTOPOL

Eye Associates of Sebastopol is the center of a vision, one which began to take form more than 30 years ago, in the heart and mind of Tamara C. Suslov, M.D. At the end of the century, with Dr. Suslov having become one of the leading eye surgeons in the nation, that vision has extended around the world.

Born in Yugoslavia to Russian parents who fled the revolution after her grandfather was killed, Tamara, along with her mother, was forced to flee Yugoslavia in 1953, entering a refugee camp in Italy. She had begun her first year of medical school in Yugoslavia and continued her medical education at the refugee camp, learning laboratory skills at a local hospital. After immigrating to the United States, she learned English and put herself through college at the University of California, Berkeley and through medical school at the University of California School of Medicine, San Francisco, (UCSF) earning her M.D. degree in 1964.

She was the first female resident in the UCSF General Surgery Department and the second female

Dr. Tamara Suslov at her Sonoma County Home.

resident in the Ophthalmology Department. After opening Eye Associates in Sebastopol, she remained on the teaching staff at UCSF, and is still an associate clinical professor of ophthalmology at that institution.

Dr. Suslov opened her ophthalmology practice in Sebastopol in 1971, in a building just north of Palm Drive Hospital. This office was offered to her by hospital administration, to entice her come

to Sebastopol and become the very first specialist in town. The practice grew rapidly in the early 1980s, drawing patients from throughout northern California and eventually from around the world. Dr. Suslov and her staff have treated people from such diverse places as New Zealand, Japan, Nicaragua, Switzerland and Saudi Arabia.

In the years that followed, Eye Associates added satellite offices in order to provide patients with care closer to their homes. The doctors saw this as a particularly important issue for senior patients with visual difficulties faced with driving long distances. Eye Associates opened facilities in Santa Rosa in 1984, Clearlake in 1986, San Francisco in 1987 and Sonoma in 1991. The San Francisco office closed in 1994 due to the intrusion of managed care.

Emphasizing the belief that services should be conveniently and expertly provided, Eye Associates offered outpatient surgery, free transportation, extended hours, and a physician that was always on call.

In 1987, Eye Associates built the Sebastopol Eye Center immediately south of Palm Drive Hospital. The center was built to house a medical eye clinic and an ambulatory surgery center dedicated to providing state-of-the-art, affordable, accessible, and safe eye care. The most modern and advanced ophthalmic equipment was purchased for the center.

Congressman Dr. William Fillante was the keynote speaker at the grand opening of the Eye Center. This was a proud moment for Dr. Suslov, who had succeeded in combining the highest technology with the most personal patient care.

Noting that eye surgery is highly stressful, despite its excellent statistical safety, Dr. Suslov added, "We can do more to alleviate a patient's anxiety here in our

Sebastopol Eye Center - 11,500 square-foot facility for total eye care.

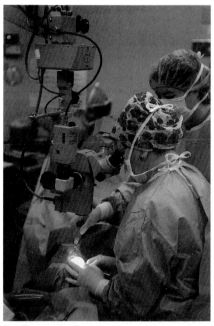

Dr. Tamara Suslov in surgery with operating microscope.

outpatient setting, since our nurses and staff are specifically trained in the care of eye surgery patients."

The combined Sebastopol Eye Center staff grew to around 40, including eye physicians and surgeons, optometrists, nurses, technicians, opticians, and administrative staff—all dedicated to the care and welfare of the patients. The organization pledged:

• To do everything possible to offer the most advanced techniques, using the most modern medical equipment available.

• To use every possible method to accurately predict the outcome for each procedure, avoiding making promises that could not be kept.

• To remember the personal and emotional needs of the patients and to meet these needs whenever possible, answering questions simply, completely and promptly.

• To maintain clean, comfortable and convenient facilities.

• To do everything possible to control the cost of care.

• To deliver 100% and do so courteously, admitting when efforts were less than perfect and making amends.

The surgery center was equipped to perform all major eye surgeries and was certified by Medicare and the State of California to perform all ambulatory surgery procedures. This was the only full-service eye center in the North Bay/North Coast area and was among the first 10% of facilities in the United States to perform phaco-emulsification surgery for cataracts. The center pioneered the use of the YAG laser for treatment of secondary cataracts and other diseases. This laser joined the argon laser, used in the treatment of glaucoma and diseases of the iris and retina, and a krypton laser, used for treatment of retinal diseases, diabetes, and vascular conditions.

The center offered cataract surgery, lens implants, cryosurgery for retinal detachment, corneal transplants, refractive surgery, a variety of laser procedures, and oculoplastic surgery.

With the help of sophisticated equipment, the doctors developed

a reputation for performing thorough medical evaluations and accurate diagnoses.

At the same time, Eye Associates instituted wide-ranging educational programs designed to raise public awareness of eye diseases and their symptoms, so that people would seek treatment in a timely fashion.

In keeping with Dr. Suslov's vision, Eye Associates opened its facilities to everyone whose sight could benefit from the skills of its staff and the quality of its equipment and procedures.

From the beginning, they participated in the National Eye Care Project which was started in 1986 by the American Academy of Ophthalmology. This program helped to connect the disadvantaged elderly, who tend to suffer most from eye disease, with physicians who volunteered their services.

In 1993, after the death of her mother, Dr.Suslov donated her mother's estate to form a charitable organization dedicated to the preservation of sight throughout the world. This organization was named Vision International-Eye

Dr. Usha and Dr. Kim from Aravind Eye Hospital visiting Sebastopol Eye Center.

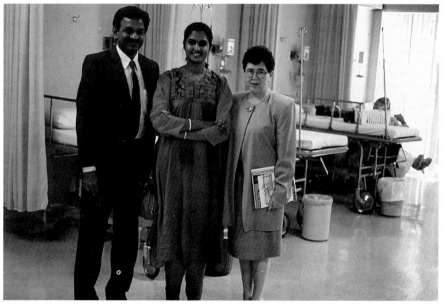

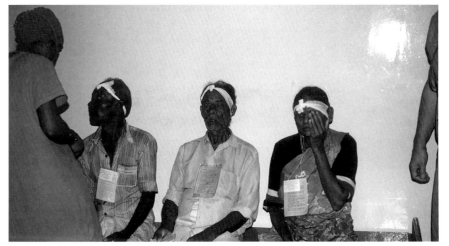

Dr. Paul Suslov and Dr. Tamara Suslov in India. Patients being readied for surgery.

Missions and represented the rest of Dr. Suslov's dream of extending eye care to countries where physicians and equipment were scarce or nonexistent. The mission of Vision International is to train and assist ophthalmologists in seriously underprivileged areas by providing them with medical education, equipment and supplies.

Dr. Suslov's daughter, Sophia Wamsley, M.D., M.P.H., serves on the board of directors of Vision International. She received her Master's degree in Public Health Ophthalmology at Johns Hopkins University in Baltimore in 1997 and her M.D. degree from Thomas Jefferson University School of Medicine in Philadelphia in 1999.

Through Vision International, doctors from several countries were brought to the Sebastopol Eye Center for training to improve their ophthalmological skills, and were sent home with equipment and supplies to establish improved eye care in their own countries.

The first physician in the program was Dr. Genady Sokolov, from the Children's Eye Surgery Center, in Orenburg, Russia. Dr. Sokolov was the only children's eye care specialist in a region with a popula-

tion so large that children alone numbered one million. Although his center treated hundreds of children, the treatment was somewhat primitive. They had no vitrectomy instruments, and didn't even have sterile eye patches. They used strips of boiled cloth for surgical dressings. Worse yet, the Orenburg Center was on the verge of being closed. Equipment and supplies donated by Vision International and the additional training the doctor received all helped to keep the center open and to improve its services, as well. Vision International has provided the same services to physicians from China, Japan, Estonia, and Madagascar.

Another Vision International project, in which Dr. Paul Suslov participated, included a humanitarian trek to Nepal. During this mission 800 people were examined,

Dr. Jean Jores Razafindrakoto and Dr. Alice Jeje Harisoa in front of the Sebastopol Eye Center.

and 160 underwent cataract surgery.

Because complete training of a new ophthalmologist for the developing world is not possible in the United States, Vision International applied to Aravind Eye Hospital, in India, for a "developing world" training program. Aravind Eye Hospital is a world-renowned model for delivery of eye care in countries such as India and Nepal and is an equally renowned training center.

Through an agreement with Aravind, Vision International sponsors two physicians for a four-year ophthalmology residency. Vision International supports the physicians by paying all expenses, including tuition. Currently, two doctors from Madagascar, Jean Jores Razafindrakoto and Alice Jeje Harisoa, are in their third year of ophthalmology residency at Aravind. Upon completion of the program, Vision International will assist them in opening an eye clinic in Madagascar, where there are currently only two ophthalmologists caring for 12 million inhabitants.

Eye Associates has recently acquired a powerful partner, Dr. Eric J. Kahle, who shares the visions for both Eye Associates and Vision International.

At the center of all this activity has been Dr. Tamara Suslov, herself. This pioneering woman and nationally-recognized expert has been a prolific educator and speaker, having presented numerous papers on medical and surgical procedures in ophthalmology. She was among the first ophthalmic surgeons to operate with the aid of microscopes and to use a wide range of other techniques and equipment.

Combining her passions for education and technology with her world vision, Dr. Suslov has created an organization that has truly made a difference, not only for Sonoma County, but for the world.

GENERAL HYDROPONICS, INC.

In the mid-1970s, a group of scientists, engineers and technicians came together with a common goal, to advance agricultural technology by a quantum leap; together they created General Hydroponics Company. Now, over 25 years later, General Hydroponics is a leading innovator in the field of hydroponics, with factories in Sebastopol, California and in southern France.

Recognizing a global need for new technology to feed an exploding human population, General Hydroponics has developed and offers leading-edge agricultural technology throughout the world. Clients ranging from home gardeners, students and scientists use General Hydroponics products to cultivate plants in enriched nutrient solutions without soil. In regions as diverse as the U.S. Antarctic research station to the hot arid deserts of the Middle East, General Hydroponics products grow plants where they have never grown before.

General Hydroponics' company goal is to enable hydroponic cultivation of top-quality crops. Hydro-

ponics has long been recognized as the technical means for cultivating crops under controlled conditions. This has enabled cultivation year-round and in extreme environments. For example, NASA uses General Hydroponics products for research in preparation for cultivation on the International Space Station.

The greater challenge, however, has been to cultivate gourmet-quality produce hydroponically. Many years of work have gone into developing specialized fertilizers enabling gourmet quality crops to be grown hydroponically. In the late 1980s General Hydroponics developed the "Flora" line of nutrients, leading to the cultivation of fruits and vegetables which rivaled "organically" grown produce for flavor and nutrition. Selected by the top gourmet restaurants in the San Francisco Bay area, produce grown using General Hydroponics technology proved superior in quality to any previously-grown hydroponic produce.

No longer a novelty, hydroponic produce is offered today at markets throughout the world and is often selected by discriminating consumers as the preferred produce. In Australia, hydroponics is synonymous

General Hydroponics founder Lawrence Brooke demonstrates a tomato crop growing in an "AeroFlo" system in the 10,000 square-foot greenhouse at Sebastopol headquarters. Each plant grows within a 3-inch diameter cup;, roots descend into a flowing stream of enriched nutrient solution. Growth rate and yield in this hydroponic system is about one third greater than can be achieved in soil. The flavor of this produce is equal to the finest organically grown produce.

with superior quality over conventionally grown produce. Giant factory farms in Canada grow fruits, flowers and vegetables to meet their domestic need as well as for export south into the enormous United States market. Hydroponic produce has been a mainstay of the European diet for over 30 years. Israeli scientists have pushed the edge on hydroponic technology for 25 years, and have developed the most advanced systems in the field of hydroponics. Collaboration between General Hydroponics scientists and leading Israeli scientists has enabled General Hydroponics to ride the crest of the wave as a technical leader in commercializing hydroponic systems and fertilizers. To learn more about General Hydroponics and the rapidly developing field of hydroponics see www.generalhydroponics.com.

Nestled amongst the rolling hills of Sonoma County, General Hydroponics' Sebastopol facility manufactures hydroponic systems and fertilizers for the North American market. The company facility includes a traditional vegetable farm as well as greenhouses for hydroponic cultivation. By growing crops in "Gold Ridge" soil as well as in the greenhouses, a comparison of growth rates, yields and quality is achieved. Luther Burbank called Sonoma County the most perfect place on Earth to grow plants. The natural farm at General Hydroponics provides a rigorous challenge to the hydroponic farm.

GROSKOPF-WEIDER TRUCKING CO., INC.

For over 95 years, the Groskopf family has been a part of Sonoma Valley history. Both Charles E. Groskopf and Lena K. Groskopf were born and raised in the valley. They married in 1919 and their son was born on Christmas day, 1920. In l939, Charles E. Groskopf and his son, Charles J. Groskopf started a small trucking company under the name of Charles E. Groskopf & Son. They started out by hauling cattle to the market in San Francisco, gravel and rock to various destinations in the valley, wild horses out of the State of Nevada to Petaluma and hay from Isleton and Merced to various ranches in the Bay Area.

In 1944, Charles J. Groskopf married Doris M. Rude, and they both worked in the trucking business. From this union they had three children—a son, Ronald, and two daughters, Charlene and Barbara. They built their home on land owned by the Groskopf Family and still live there, some 54 years later.

In l946 Charles J. Groskopf brought in Stewart R. Weider as a business partner, changing the business name to Groskopf-Weider Trucking Company. They bought their first 18-wheeler in 1946 and began hauling lumber out of Ft. Bragg and Willits. In 1947 they purchased another tractor, which they used to log for Willits Redwood Products. In the early '50s, Groskopf-Weider Trucking was the prime carrier for Sonoma Plywood and the Pacific Coast Lumber Company in Sonoma. Both were plywood manufacturers, and Groskopf-Weider hauled the veneer into the plants from Cloverdale and Crescent City and other points on the Redwood Highway. They also hauled the finished product to points in California and Nevada.

In the early '50s they developed

Charles E. Groskopf, left, and his son Charles J. Groskopf.

a leasing company with approximately 20 tractors and trailers leased out to various building supply businesses. In 1956, Groskopf-Weider bought out Blakely and Son, a petroleum

Charles J. Groskopf, left, and Charles E. Groskopf in 1939.

hauler from Modesto. They then incorporated and created three distinct businesses, all in l956: Groskopf-Weider Trucking Company, Inc.; G-W Tank Lines, Inc.; and Groskopf-Weider Leasing Company, a partnership. For some 30+ years G-W Tanks Lines serviced the petroleum accounts of Chevron and Union Oil Company.

In 1968, the Groskopf's began serving the wine industry. Sebastiani Winery became one of their first customers, a relationship that continues today. Groskopf-Weider Trucking Co., Inc. still serves the wine industry and is well known for its service and handling of wines throughout the State of California.

In 1976, following Stewart Weider's death, the Groskopf family purchased his share of the business from his family. The name remained the same for the trucking company.

In the early '80s, the Groskopf family added a wine storage warehouse and a domestic interstate/ intrastate shipping service. The original warehouse was 102,000 square-feet of space. An additional 87,000 square-feet were added in the early 1990s and 40,000 square-feet in the late '90s, expanding the company's total storage capacity to approximately 229,000 square-feet of storage, or 1.3 million cases.

The Groskopf family companies—Groskopf-Weider Trucking Co., Inc., Groskopf Warehouse and Groskopf Logistic Services are among the top 300 companies in Sonoma County and the largest storage, transportation and distribution facilities in Sonoma Valley. The company stores, consolidates and ships over 7 million cases of wine, annually.

Today, Groskopf-Weider Trucking Co., Inc. supports the warehouse by being the in-house carrier. In addition, GWT is the foremost carrier in California of bulk imported and exported wine from

Below
A portion of the fleet of tractors of Groskopf Weider Trucking Co., Inc.

Above
Left to right: Charlene Groskopf, Doris Groskopf and Barbara Groskopf-Smith.

California to all points in the world.

In 1996, Groskopf Enterprises, a holding company for the businesses, was formed. On May 12, 1998, Charles J. Groskopf passed away. Shortly after his death, his wife and widow took control of the business upon the resignation of their son, Ronald S. Groskopf. The companies are now run by Doris M. Groskopf, Charlene Groskopf and Barbara Groskopf-Smith.

The main offices are at 20580 8th Street East, Sonoma, California, but the truck terminal is still at the same Denmark Street location the family has owned for over 95 years.

KOMAG MATERIAL TECHNOLOGY

Nestled between the Russian River and luscious miles of vineyards lies one busy, hustling and bustling hi-tech company. Komag Material Technology (KMT) employs close to 200 people committed to continuously improving the company and ensuring that KMT thrives in Sonoma County for years to come.

It's a highly competitive world out there; for hi-tech companies, it's cut-throat. That why KMT in Santa Rosa works so hard to stay on the cutting edge.

Working closely with the other sites that make up Komag, Inc., (including a site in San Francisco and two sites in Malaysia—in Penang and Kuching), KMT is open 24-hours-a- day, seven-days-a-week, to develop and produce thin-film media, better known as disks.

At KMT, engineers and manufacturing operators work together to produce the first stage of Komag Inc.'s product—an aluminum substrate disk. The process is highly automated. The goal is to keep the disks out of the hands of human beings and in the trusty hands of robots. This helps keep product damage down and profits up.

Once KMT's process is complete, the disks are shipped to another Komag facility where the process is completed. The disks are sold to drive makers, and eventually end up in computers worldwide, help-

Utilizing Self-Directed Work Teams, KMT operates seven days a week, 24 hours a day to meet customer demand.

ing to store more data than ever before possible.

The Secret to KMT's Success—Its People! KMT's success is not just about technology. It's also about the company as a whole—the people, the teams, and the leaders. To stay on top, KMT makes sure the company machine is well-oiled and fine-tuned.

Robots are nice, but people still have to know how to run them. KMT regularly trains manufacturing operators to keep their skills and process knowledge high. The more employees know about and understand the process, the more they can contribute to improving it and KMT.

Aside from process training, each employee at KMT receives training in Stephen Covey's *Seven Habits of Highly Effective People*, as well as leadership series and communication seminars. KMT empowers all employees to always contribute and lead when they can.

Speaking of leaders, KMT has a Leadership Council made up of the

"People are the source of our company's intelligence, ideas, initiative, and leadership."— excerpt from Komag Material Technology's mission statement.

company's managers. These leaders work together to strategically plan how to make the best use of the company's resources—both its people and its machines. The Council works to provide direction, opportunity and support to all KMT employees.

Success isn't an individual achievement—it's due to teams of people who pool their talents and resources. Like the Leadership Council, KMT has other teams that focus on goals and work together to achieve them.

KMT helped lead the industry in creating and implementing Self-Directed Work Teams (SDWTs). Other groups focus on process improvements, as well as continuously working to promote a dynamic company culture.

You gotta have a life outside of work... People have families and hobbies and goals that have nothing to do with work. KMT understands this and encourages employees to explore the world around them.

One benefit popular with KMT's employees is tuition reimbursement. KMT not only pays tuition for its employees, but also pays for books. Employees don't have to take physics to get reimbursed. Some employees take piano and swimming lessons! The classes don't have to relate with their jobs—it's about personal growth.

Employees aren't the only ones encouraged to educate themselves at KMT. In addition to each KMT employee being allocated money each year for education, each child of a KMT employee is eligible for scholarships for higher learning.

With benefits like these, and a company focused on its people, employees don't want to leave! That's why attrition is so low, at 3%, annually.

Companies aren't "born" like this... When Komag, Inc. bought Disk Material Technology in 1988 and renamed it Komag Material Technology, both the technology and the people involved were different. Then, in 1989, Tim Starkey arrived from San Jose and started the process of turning KMT into an incredibly fun, collaborative, innovative and profitable company.

An electrical engineer, Tim was able to combine his technical expertise with his strong leadership abilities. Having confidence in Tim, employees gained increased confidence in and loyalty to KMT.

The process looks nothing like it did back then. Manufacturing operators no longer clean every disk by hand or keep notes on reams of paper. Technology has advanced, and with it, KMT's process. In 1998, KMT produced 23 times the number of disks produced in 1989. With the same number of employees, the disks produced in 1998

were much more advanced in technology and complexity.

The company culture is incredible, as well. KMT employs many members of families, and in turn has become a family itself.

There's really no secret to this success—just good, common sense. People are supported. Triumphs are shared. And, KMT continues to thrive.

Above and bottom: ISO 9002 certified since 1997, KMT credits its success to a collaborative team environment and employees dedicated to producing the highest quality product in the market.

HOP KILN WINERY, INC.

Aging Well—With Complexity. A life well-lived is much like a wine well-made, and Dr. Martin Griffin is proof. At 78, Dr. Griffin is aging well and is a pleasure to be around. His vintage is showing complexity at several levels. He is a physician (retired) with an additional Masters in Public Health, who, for 15 years pioneered a program that virtually eradicated hepatitis B in state hospitals. He is also Hop Kiln Winery's owner, an active environmentalist, and most recently, the author of *Saving the Marin-Sonoma Coast.*

Thinking he could retire as a "gentleman farmer" on the 260-acre sheep ranch he purchased in 1961, Dr. Griffin moved there in 1974. "It was so expensive starting a winery, I had to go back to work," he laughs, referring to the massive restoration of the old, three-tower hop kiln that made his property a local land-mark.

Eco-Friendly Winegrowing. As major forces in the successful preservation of some 4,000 acres of headlands in

Dr. Martin Griffin, owner of Hop Kiln Winery.

Marin and Sonoma counties, Dr. Griffin and his wife Joyce are dedicated environmentalists who have consistently strived for an eco-friendly winery. They, along with others, are establishing a 500-acre forested corridor from the Russian River to preserve the watershed called Griffin Creek and

to restore the spawning territory of the steelhead trout. Hop Kiln is a "fish-friendly farmer," holding its vineyards   back 500 feet from the river to prevent erosion and enable it to meander.

Most Photographed Building in Sonoma County. History is center stage at Hop Kiln Winery, established in 1975. The massive hop kiln that is the winery's namesake is a National, County and State Historic Landmark and has some of the county's earliest vineyards. Largely due to Dr. Griffin's efforts Westside Road was designated as a County Scenic Corridor, and his Victorian house is a County Historic Landmark. With its three-foot thick stone walls, the hop kiln is a perfect place for winemaking.

Currently, Hop Kiln produces Zinfandel, Chardonnay, Primitivo Zinfandel, Riesling and Valdigui along with the popular blends, "A Thousand Flowers" and "Marty Griffin's Big Red."

Winemaker Steve Strobl joined Hop Kiln in 1984, along with wife Jo-Anne as business and sales manager. Steve doubles as vineyard overseer and is excited about Hop Kiln's recent addition of six acres of Pinot Noir to its 40+ acres of estate vineyards.

In 1993, Hop Kiln was awarded the "Golden Winery of the Year" Award at the California State Fair for winning the most Gold Medals. Wine lovers know that Hop Kiln is producing between 8,000-10,000 cases of great wines made with respect for the wilderness and wildlife of Sonoma County, each year.

Hop Kiln invites visitors to stop by between 10:00 am-5:00 pm seven-days-a-week. The tasting room, picnic grounds and lake have repeatedly been chosen as one of the Top Ten Tasting Rooms in the wine country.

Hop Kiln Winery at Griffin Vineyard, 6050 Westside Road, Healdsburg.

MARTINI & PRATI WINERY

Sonoma County's Link to California Winemaking History. We all talk about family traditions, but few of us get to embrace the duties and rewards of a family tradition four and five generations in the making. This is the quest of the Martini's with the Martini & Prati winery. Five generations of the Martini family have been grounded in the same location, shared the same memories and aspirations, the same sweat of their brow and the same will of their hearts. Their lives have been woven in the rich history of Sonoma County viticulture. At present, their wine production serves as a bridge to the past and the future with their current production of Cal-Itals, Italian grape varieties grown here in California.

It all began nearly a century ago, when Rafael Martini came from Lucca, in Italy, and began his farm in California. Rafael grew the typical brussel sprouts, artichokes and broccoli, but held fast to the fervent dream of growing grapes. With the success of his vegetable farm, he headed north to a site closely resembling his native Tuscany—Sonoma County—and began his long-held wish of entering the wine business.

With the purchase of the Twin

Cellar workers enjoy the fruits of their labors (circa, 1910).

Elmo Martini, third-generation winemaker, in 1945.

Fir Winery in 1902, Rafael sold most of his production in bulk barrels, with the rest going to consumers who showed up at the door with jug in hand. Indeed, today visitors to Martini & Prati are invited to fill a jug of red wine directly from a barrel inside the winery. The annual "Jug Party" draws hundreds, old and young, to enjoy the age-old Italian tradition of friends, family, and wine.

Most of America's young wine industry was shut down with Prohibition in 1920. Ever the survivor, the R. Martini Wine Company took advantage of a loophole in the Volstead Act, converting their wine production to making sacramental wine and shipping almost 10,000 gallons of wine a year between 1920 and 1933. Rafael's grandson Elmo, is quoted as saying, "It's amazing how many more rabbis there suddenly were in New York during Prohibition."

In Elmo's time, the busy tasting room was full of local Italian immigrants and visitors who traveled long and far to taste their wines—a constant party of people filling jugs, telling tales, and sharing the camaraderie of the local farmers. The current tasting room was originally a stable and bunkhouse for the Italian immigrants who were housed there while working the grape crush. It is now called "Elmo's Groceria," and features walls lined with photographs from family history, and shelves filled with items and foodstuffs related to the Italian tradition. Visitors can tour the winery with its historic 35,000 gallon redwood tanks, built in 1943, and the concrete fermentation tanks, all still used today.

"Martini & Prati portrays California winemaking history – a heritage that should be remembered," says Tom Martini, Elmo'son. "Our legacy is so rich that we wish to preserve it for others to understand and enjoy. The old redwood tanks represent a lost art. A cellar with wooden tanks holds the secrets of the past." It is clearly Tom's and his brother Jim's intent to restore and maintain traditions, and to pass along the richly woven stories to the next generation.

For Martini & Prati, family heritage is the theme of the winery, and they feel a deep sense of purpose. The goal of the Martini family is to be considered among the best Cal-Ital wine producers in Sonoma County. They offer a destination for those interested in the rich California wine history. According to the family matriarch Harriet Martini, "The winery has always been the pride and joy of our family. We intend to advance in the direction of maintaining our tradition, while building our future. Elmo would be honored by the ongoing, forward movement to maintain our place in the Sonoma wine industry."

MAX MACHINERY, INC.

Max Machinery was founded in a small shop in Lafayette, on the Eastern side of the San Francisco Bay, in 1966. Working as a designer and service technician for a manufacturer of urethane foams and dispensing equipment, John Max gained exposure to the manufacture of mixing and dispensing machines. When the company he was working for decided that small machinery didn't fit into their product line, John set off to develop and sell mixing machinery on his own.

Urethanes are two component (or more) compounds which, when combined at the proper ratios, form a solid or a foam with the desired physical characteristics. The industry was born in the 1940s and has quietly grown to touch the daily lives of just about everyone. The urethanes are used as foam for auto bumpers, seats and furniture. As solids, they are used for items such as in-line skate wheels, golf balls,

paper mill rolls, office printer rolls and medical products.

Some of the first dispensing machines that Max Machinery made were used for encapsulating electronic components. Later, specializing in machines for solid (i.e., non-form) parts led the company into tackling more difficult projects, such as clear urethane for aircraft windshields, bubble-free pours for medical products and high-value printing rollers.

Scale and complexity of the blending machines increased as Max was asked to create solutions to blend more difficult chemicals. In 1970, the company moved north to Healdsburg. With five employees from Lafayette, John Max set up shop in a vacant bowling alley on the north end of town, becoming an early cornerstone of the technology base of Sonoma County. The company uses many local suppliers, several founded by previous employees, helping to develop technologically-based businesses in what had been a predominately agricul-

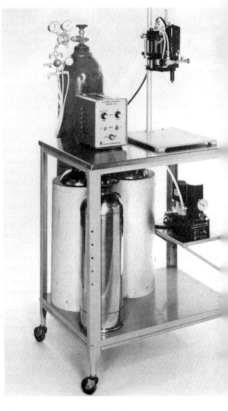

Early, two chemical blending system.

tural and lumber-based economy. Likewise, the company has made an effort to support the sciences and skilled trades at area schools by providing machinery and grants to several local schools.

From the original five employees, the Healdsburg staff has grown to approximately 70 employees, yet still maintains a low profile. About 80% of its sales are in the U.S., of which less than 5% on average are in California. Max extends a lifetime commitment to all of its customers—now including those in Europe, South America, India, Japan and Australia—providing technical service, repairs and spare parts for even their oldest machines. Max Machinery's record of success in solving difficult urethane challenges, keeps California and Sonoma County on the minds of the urethane industry.

Current, computer controlled dispensing system.

MONITOR PUBLISHING

Building a network of Internet computers was no problem for the founders of Monitor Publishing in 1995—their real problems began when they had to relearn how to use a typewriter.

"All of the legal documents had to be typed," laughs co-founder Jeff Elliott. "But neither of us had touched a typewriter for over a decade. It took us all day to fill out the forms; we were scared to death of the thing." Typed (very slowly) on those pages, however, was their terse company mission statement: Quality Internet access and journalism in service of the community.

"Non-profit and community groups stood to benefit most from being on-line," co-founder Darryl Trujillo recalls. "We spent much of

Young families and seniors benefit most from Internet access, but are often intimidated by the technology. Monitor's personalized service gives them the confidence they need.

our first year explaining how the Internet could help even the smallest organizations." Monitor also began an outreach to senior citizens and residents of rural West County. "That first stage of the Internet revolution was bypassing these groups," says Trujillo. "Many hadn't used a computer before, or found that their only choice for Internet access was a long-distance call to Santa Rosa. Others were intimidated because they didn't know anyone already on-line, and worried that using the Internet could somehow get them into trouble."

Trujillo and Elliott soon noticed that they were part of a "virtual" community. "We've known many of our customers for years via e-mail and telephone," Elliott says. Most of their customers, however, they've never met in person. The two men also found that almost all new

customers were coming from referrals from current Monitor users. "It's become like an extended family," Truillo believes. "If a customer in Bodega Bay is having computer problems, for example, we can usually suggest a neighbor that might be able to help them."

Besides making sure that the Internet service runs smoothly, Elliott and Trujillo also produce the on-line newspaper, *Albion Monitor*. One of the very first news publications available on the web, it now has an international readership. Elliott explains why: "Our motto is 'The News You're Missing' — these are important articles or commentaries overlooked by the media at large. Also, the *Albion Monitor* is unique: we draw from sources in both the 'alternative' and mainstream press, allowing us to choose from a wide variety of material."

The *Albion Monitor* also publishes Simone Wilson's popular "Footprints" series. In each article, Wilson explores an event in North Bay history combined with a detailed hike or walk at the location where the story occurred.

But why the name "Albion" Monitor? "It's poetic, not geographic," Elliott explains. "Sir Francis Drake landed on our coast in 1579 and called this wonderful place 'Nova Albion.' Drake and his ship's crew were respectful of the land and its people; there's no proven trace of his visit. We use the name Albion to remind us that like Drake, we're also visitors here in Eden."

POMEROY CORPORATION

The roots of Pomeroy Corporation can be traced back to the early industrial development of this country and free enterprise. The infrastructure of our country has evolved due to the vision and ingenuity of such men as John H. (Jack) Pomeroy and Ben C. Gerwick. These pioneers were early American entrepreneurs and the initial founders of Pomeroy Corporation.

John H. (Jack) Pomeroy was a self-educated, self-made man. In 1915, he started his own business in the field of heavy construction. As the country grew, his company was there to provide expertise in the construction of dams, bridges, hydro-electric plants, highways, railways and seaports.

By contrast, Ben C. Gerwick was a college graduate with a degree in civil engineering. He went to work as a civil engineer for Western Pacific Railroad. Later, he worked with Ernest L. Ransome, who had developed the unit system of precast concrete construction. During the installation of the Hetch Hetchy Pipeline, Ben Gerwick designed, constructed and patented the Hetch Hetchy Caisson. This patented method was later used during the construction of the center pier of the Golden Gate Bridge.

In February 1926, Ben C. Gerwick, Inc. was founded. In the beginning, Ben C. Gerwick, Inc. constructed bridge trestles, ferry slips, wharves and industrial foundations; later there were government contracts for the military. Ben C. Gerwick, Inc. was twice awarded the Army-Navy "E" award.

Ben C. Gerwick, Inc. helped pioneer the prestressed concrete industry in the United States. In 1945, 100 acres of land on the Petaluma River, south of Petaluma, was purchased in order to manufacture precast concrete piles. The first prestressing bed was designed and

Pomeroy Corporation's main office and manufacturing plant in Petaluma, California.

built in the Petaluma yard in 1954.

In 1958, these two heavy construction pioneer groups joined their expertise. Both groups benefited. Pomeroy benefited from Gerwick's expertise in the prestressed concrete operation for foundation work, and Gerwick from the greater opportunity to acquire overseas work as a result of the joint venture with Pomeroy.

The Petaluma precast/prestressed plant is presently known as Pomeroy Corporation. Since 1958, the Petaluma facility has undergone a number of corporate changes. However, it has been constant in the manufacture of precast/prestressed concrete products. In 1995, Pomeroy Corporation became part of the Morrison Knudsen Corporation.

The contribution that Pomeroy and Gerwick made to the massive infrastructure and transportation system of this country is their legacy.

As the 21st century dawned, these massive structures required maintenance and upgrading. Pomeroy Corporation again plays a major role in the retrofitting, upgrading and expansion of these vital systems.

Pomeroy Corporation's base of operation is ideally located on the Petaluma River. The river serves as a means of transportation for the manufactured product. The Petaluma plant site has access to the entire Bay Area and all of the West Coast. Pomeroy Corporation is primarily a manufacturing plant, specializing in precast/prestressed concrete products, including bridge components, building systems, piling, and railroad crossties. To date over 250,000 crossties have been used on the Bay Area Rapid

Transit (BART) system; the 5'6" gauge ties were designed to meet BART specifications. A large percentage of Pomeroy Corporation's work is for Caltrans and other public works agencies.

To manufacture a prestressed product requires that high strength steel cables (that have already been stressed) be cast into the concrete product as reinforcement. Precast means that the product is cast and manufactured at a base of operations, and later transported to the installation site.

There is a constant evolution of products due to advanced technology. The manufacture of precast/prestressed concrete products must be adjusted to meet new codes and guidelines for earthquake resistance.

For over 50 years, Pomeroy Corporation has been an integral part of the business community of Petaluma. They have contributed significantly to the economy, making every effort to keep the money within the community, by accommodating the local business

community. They have a stable workforce of approximately 100 employees, many of whom are long-term, and even second generation employees. Much of the success of Pomeroy Corporation is attributed to the solid core of focused employees who understand the techniques required for the manufacture of precast/prestressed concrete products.

Currently, Pomeroy Corporation is manufacturing seismic restraining collars (nicknamed "dog-bones") as part of the retrofitting of the San Mateo Bridge. Another major project in process is San Francisco's new baseball stadium. Pomeroy Corporation has nearly completed manufacturing the seat risers in the stadium. Among other recently completed projects are the San Leandro outfall sewer system, the Oakland Coliseum Arena and the aerial girders for the BART extension in Concord.

During the summer of 1999, Pomeroy Corporation expanded its precast/prestressed manufacturing operation into southern California. The first manufacturing contract was for the upgrading of the Alameda Corridor rail transportation system in Los Angeles.

Another project in which Pomeroy Corporation takes great pride is the Sunshine Skyway Bridge over Florida's Tampa Bay. It is one of the largest precast segmental bridges in the United States, and one of the longest cable-stayed bridges in the world. There are times when it is more economically feasible to set up a temporary manufacturing site on location; the Sunshine Skyway is an example. In 1983, Pomeroy Corporation obtained a contract to manufacture all of the precast concrete components that, when joined together, composed the entire structure of the bridge. Rather than try to manufacture the pieces at their

Precast seat riser installation at the new San Francisco Giants baseball stadium—1999.

plant in Petaluma, Pomeroy sent a crew down to Tampa Bay to set up a temporary site in Port Manatee, Florida. More than 200 employees were hired for the casting job. The precast segments were built at the Port Manatee site, barged to the bridge site and lifted into place. The project was completed in five years.

Pomeroy Corporation has long supported its local community. Youth and the schools are first and foremost in the company's priorities. Other projects include hospice and the community drug programs. Pomeroy Corporation is an active member of the Petaluma Chamber of Commerce.

Pomeroy Corporation's philosophy is to support the professional growth and development of each individual employee, through continuous education. Education and respect of each person builds a strong family of employees. With a strong workforce, Pomeroy Corporation is able to continue pursuing broader markets in the future.

Sunshine Skyway Bridge, Tampa Bay, Florida, 1987.

SERRES CORPORATION, SERRES RANCH & SERRES VINEYARDS

Along the west side of Highway 12, a few miles north of the town of Sonoma, lies what appears to be a well-kept ranch with luscious green vineyards enclosed by neat white-washed fences. The mailbox beside the road reads "Serres." A motorist driving Highway 12 would never guess what lies beyond the pristine setting.

The Serres Ranch was part of a square-mile grant that once belonged to Fighting Joe Hooker of Civil War fame. By the 1870s, the property passed to the Watriss family and in the early 1900s it was willed to John P. Serres, grandfather of the present John P. Serres. Still standing is Hooker's ranch house, which is presently occupied by the members of the Serres family. Although Serres was not linked by bloodlines to the Watriss family, the care with which he had managed the Watriss lands and ranching operation resulted in his being designated heir to the Watriss property.

In 1929, John P. Serres started a gravel-processing operation and began to sell aggregate. The business grew during the Depression, when the WPA projects generated a great demand for its products.

John P. Serres was an outgoing man who served as road master for Sonoma County, member of the election committee, fire marshal, and trustee on the local school board. Along with his work as a gravel-processing operator and his various civic responsibilities, Serres also managed to supervise the large-scale dairy operation that was begun by Hooker and continued by the Watrisses.

The business took on a very different style when John's son, Frank took over the family ranch

The Serres family: Judy and John Serres, and children Buck, 12, Taylor, 9, and John, 15.

and the gravel-processing business. Frank was less outgoing than his father. But he, too, was linked to the past by a life that began and ended in the old ranch house that had been built long before Fighting Joe Hooker. The bond between the Watriss and Serres families was passed down through successive generations. The story is told of how Frank was originally given the name John Marshall Serres. When he was 3 years old, Frank discarded this name and chose Franklin Watriss Serres as his new name. From that day on, Frank was known as Franklin Watriss Serres in honor of the family that was intertwined with his own.

During the early 1950s Frank built from scratch his own rock-crushing and ready-mix plant, in addition to supplying the paving materials for other contractors. Frank involved his own company in the heavy construction business. A significant part of Serres Construction at that time involved road construction. As the number of cars in Sonoma County multiplied, there was a greater need

for strong, smoothly paved public roads. Old timers around the Sonoma Valley have often commented, "any road that Frank Serres built is still there." Frank was also skilled as a metal fabricator.

During the years that Frank Serres ran the business, the company supplied concrete for several large projects, including the Hannah Boys Center and the Bank of America in Sonoma. Serres constructed new roads such as Armstrong Grove Road, Madrone Road, Arnold Drive, and London Ranch Road.

When Frank died in 1974, his son, current owner John P. Serres, was barely 20 years old. With his arm in a cast after a calf roping accident took his thumb, he took over the company. A cousin, Shorty Mills, who had recently broken a leg, helped with the start-up. John laughs when he thinks back on the two young men who, between the two of them, only "added up to a man and a half." Nevertheless, in spite of his youth and a temporary handicap, John managed the transition.

By 1974 the construction phase of the company had slowed down in preparation to enlarge the ready-mix division. Since his father had already reduced the size of the construction crew, John was afforded the flexibility to develop the business along the lines he saw fit. John chose to increase paving. His firm used to do the majority of private work in the Sonoma area. Although the company has grown significantly during the years since 1974, most of its projects are within a 25-mile radius of Sonoma.

In 1988, John Serres decided he would buy back a portion of the original Serres ranch, which now had grapes planted on it. He suddenly found himself in the wine business, supplying his high-quality red fruit to many local wineries. John has developed most of Serres Ranch into vineyards and is currently farming 150 acres of red grapes. He also manages to bottle a few cases of his homemade special Zinfandel, Cabernet Franc, Cab Sav and Merlot, which has awarded him many medals at the Santa Rosa Harvest Fair.

Along with Serres Corporation and Serres Vineyards, John also keeps a cattle operation going in Laytonville, CA.

Serres Corporation is currently managed by John and his wife Judy Serres. Together they run the construction company, cattle and vineyard businesses. Katherine Serres, "Katie," John's mother, was an integral part of the business until she passed away in December 1995. She is missed by her family, friends and espe-

Left to right: James Morgan, Frank Serres, and Bill Hamburg in an early 1930s photo taken at the gravel bunkers at Serres Ranch.

cially her grandchildren.

Serres Corporation contributes to a variety of local efforts. Serres has donated labor and materials to projects at almost every school in Sonoma Valley, with larger projects like the Sonoma Valley High School track and the parking lot at Sonoma Community Center. Of special interest to the Serres Corporation are projects that encourage or serve the children of the area, like the Field of Dreams, Maxwell Park's Baseball Fields, Katie's Field (named after his mother), and currently the Sonoma Skate Park.

Perhaps one reason why John Serres takes special interest in children is because he and Judy have three of their own. Two sons, John Marshall Serres and

Buchanan "Buck" Serres, and a daughter, Taylor Paige Serres, who are growing up on the same ranch where their father and grandfather spent their young years.

John Serres has a hands-on approach to his business. Although he employs around 50 people, he stays fully informed about all aspects of his company's business. He is confident that its size offers flexibility to vary with the economic trends. Serres Corporation, Serres Ranch and Serres Vineyards look forward to slow, steady growth as the needs of the community continue to change and increase.

SONOMA COUNTY MUSEUM

This impressive structure, the last of its kind, now houses the Sonoma County Museum at 425 Seventh Street in Santa Rosa. It functioned differently in the daily lives of early Sonoma County residents. From 1909 to 1966, it served as the United States Post Office and later housed Federal Offices. Originally constructed at 401 Fifth Street in Santa Rosa, the building, known as a fine example of the Spanish Renaissance Revival style was designed by the talented architect James Knox Taylor.

In 1975 the Sonoma County Bicentennial Commission recommended that a museum be established. By 1977 the operational mantle was passed to the newly incorporated Historical Museum Foundation of Sonoma County along with $80,000 raised to acquire an appropriate building to house the Museum. In 1979 when Santa Rosa downtown development became a threat to the old Post Office's existence, the building was moved from its original location to its present home. The local community paved the way for its opening in January 1985 as the Sonoma County Museum, a

The interior lobby looked much the same as it was.

Much work was required between the time the old post office building was moved to Seventh Street and the day it opened as the Sonoma County Museum in January 1985.

repository and showcase of Sonoma County history, culture, and art.

The mission of the Sonoma County Museum is to provide cultural experiences for the enrichment, enjoyment, and education of Sonoma County residents and visitors through the preservation of collections, and the presentation of exhibits and programs. Every year 15,000 visitors experience the past and present in this carefully restored structure.

The primary responsibilities of the Sonoma County Museum are to preserve, exhibit, and educate. The exhibits emphasize geographic, economic, cultural and artistic aspects of the area and the diverse cultural makeup of its population. In support of its mission, the Museum focuses on two objectives: the on-going development and maintenance of the permanent historical and early California art exhibit, and the presentation of 10 to 13 temporary exhibits per year.

History comes to life at the Museum especially for the leaders of the next millennium—the children. Each year 6,500 youngsters from every school district in the County are challenged by Museum staff and docents to become historical detectives by searching for clues in photos, flags and toys. Thus the purpose of the Museum's educational programs have been designed to deepen public understanding of the material

presented in the exhibits; to create interactive learning opportunities; and to extend the resources of the Museum beyond the physical walls of the institution to audiences who might not otherwise be able to visit.

The Sonoma County Museum is also the primary institution in the County which collects, preserves, interprets, and makes available for research historical artifacts, documents, photographs and works of art which relate to the cultural heritage of Sonoma County. The collections contain approximately 20,000 items documenting County history and culture from the time prior to European contact to the present.

The Museum is partially supported by a large and growing membership. It hosts various fund-raisers such as beer and wine tastings on an annual basis, and it has an expanding core of volunteers. As one of the stewards of Sonoma County history, Curator Evangeline Tai continuously praises those volunteers whose help is essential to the function of the Museum.

As the end of this millennium approaches, the Sonoma County Museum is going into an expansion campaign that when completed will put the Museum on the map as being the premier cultural campus in the County.

STONE CREEK WINES

Stone Creek Wines, housed in the old Kenwood schoolhouse, is home to the fifth-generation of a family-owned and operated business, the Simon Levi Company. With 125 years of experience in California business to guide them, the Jacobs family, headed by Jay Jacobs and sons Barry and Brad, has successfully transformed the Stone Creek Wine brand into a vital Sonoma County business and trendsetting winery. By blending their business policies with their special appreciation of family and history, the Jacobs have created an organization that honors the past and the present—from the charm of its schoolhouse location to its flexible, family-oriented work schedules.

Simon Levi Company began in 1873 in Temecula, California, when founder Simon Levi from Austria, opened his first general merchandise store, after years of studying English and the retail trade at night. Simon moved his business to the city of San Diego in 1876, where he proved to be a popular local figure, holding many prestigious community positions before ultimately being appointed postmaster by then President Ulysses S. Grant. In 1925, when the torch was passed to Simon's son-in-law, J.B. Jacobs who graduated high school in Antioch, the Simon Levi Company had established itself as a community and business leader in both San Diego and Los Angeles counties. By 1966, J.B.'s grandson, Jay headed the Simon Levi Company, then one of the major alcoholic beverage distributors in California. In 1989, Jay closed the distributorship and moved the Jacobs family north again, this time to establish Stone Creek Wines in the fertile Kenwood area of Sonoma County.

The family's commitment to maintaining a sense of history is reflected in their choice of location; the Old Blue Schoolhouse was built in 1890, just 17 years after their great-grandfather opened his first store. Under the fifth-generation influences of Brad and Barry, the Simon Levi Company now boasts a liberal, family-first approach to business management. Stone Creek established its core purpose of "having fun making wine that people want to drink" in the early '90s, when it pioneered the blockbuster varietal, Merlot. The Jacobs' anticipated the trend, and as a result grew the Stone Creek brand from a few thousand cases of Merlot to about 200,000 cases today.

The Jacobs' also anticipated the increasing need to adapt the work environment to the changing social needs of family life. Their customized flextime and task-driven work schedules allow employees to work at home or take time off during

Entrance to Stone Creek Wines and the tasting room, which includes a picnic area. This was formerly the Kenwood schoolhouse.

their workday to ensure a balance between their personal and professional lives. Liberal education philosophies promote personal growth and foster a supportive learning environment within the workplace. Employees are encouraged to be entrepreneurial and responsible, skills that the Jacobs' believe support the individual in their personal as well as their professional lives.

The Jacobs' feel strongly that the focus of business is giving people a good life: balanced, happy employees produce superior products and attract profitable opportunities to benefit the entire organization. They also believe Sonoma County embodies the ideal of that good life, and for the future of the upcoming sixth-generation, their customers and employees, that's important.

WEEKS DRILLING AND PUMP COMPANY

Weeks Drilling and Pump Company, formally Weeks Hardware Store, was established in 1906 by Hod Weeks, in the heart of Sebastopol, a small town west of Santa Rosa. In 1949, Walter and Mary Thompson purchased the business and retained the long-established name.

Born in 1904 in a dirt floor log cabin in Eagle, Colorado, Walter and older brother Hugh broke horses and rode the rodeo circuit in their early teens, ending up in California, where Walter met and married his wife, Mary, in 1926.

Although he had no formal education beyond the seventh grade, Walter succeeded at many business ventures, including an ice plant, a restaurant and creamery, a sawmill with 7,000 acres of timberland and home-building in Santa Rosa. In 1949, after a short retirement, Walter and Mary entered the hardware and pump business, when they purchased Weeks Hardware.

In the early '50s Walter bought a modern mud rotary drill rig, the first of its kind in the area. In 1955, he sold the hardware store and along with older sons Wayne and Jerry, concentrated on the drilling and pump business. He purchased more drill rigs, opened a branch office in Ukiah and got involved in "wildcat" oil and gas exploration in California and Nevada.

Following Walter's untimely death in 1959 at age 55, Mary joined her older sons in the business where, at age 92 she continues to

Mary and Walter Thompson in front of Weeks Hardware, circa early '50s.

Thompson family: Left to right; Ward (ADC president, 1977 & 1978), Bob, Mary (receiving Associated Drilling Contractor's "Woman of the Year Award" in 1974), Wayne, and Jerry.

play an active role today. Sons Bob and Ward entered the business in 1961 and all four brothers ran the business together for over 20 years.

In the '80s, Jerry and Wayne retired and key management employees, Charlie Hawkes, Bruce Anderson, Ray Wilson and grandson, Chris, became board members. In the '90s Bruce, Charlie, and son Bob retired, and Charlie Judson, along with grandson Rob, were elected to the board.

During the past three decades the business has continued to grow and expand to serve the Greater Bay Area, including work as far north as the Oregon border and as far south as Los Angeles. In addition to Weeks' mainstay of rural domestic and irrigation systems, the company diversified into environmental, geo-technical and water treatment, while expanding one of the largest fleets in the state.

In the '70s an excellent retirement program was implemented to benefit all employees. The Company (and many employees) also actively support community causes and local charitable organizations.

Weeks currently operates 12 drilling rigs and 11 pump rigs, and

employs over 60 personnel. Their growth can be attributed mainly to their expansion into environmental drilling and the role they have played in water development for the continually expanding winery and viticulture industries.

Weeks is truly a family business. The past 50 years have seen Mary and Walter, four sons, four daughters–in-law, a brother, and numerous grandchildren in the business, as well as many other "non-Thompson" employees with family members working together at Weeks.

Weeks' president Ward Thompson attributes the company's success to an "excellent team of long-term employees who care about the quality of their work and share the Thompson family's commitment to integrity, customer service and satisfaction." They have helped build Weeks Drilling and Pump Company into one of the largest, most respected and reliable companies in northern California.

A TIMELINE OF SONOMA COUNTY'S HISTORY

Circa 3,000 B.C.E. Native Americans (Coast Miwok, Pomo, and Wappo) take up residence in coastal terraces and oak woodlands north of San Francisco Bay.

1579 Francis Drake lands his ship *Golden Hinde* on the North Coast for five weeks in the vicinity of Drake's Bay or Bodega Bay, where the crew encounters the local Miwok and prepares for the voyage home across the Pacific.

1775 Spanish explorer Juan Bodega y Cuadra is the first European to anchor in Bodega Bay, although he does not land.

1790 English mariner James Colnett anchors in Bodega Bay, believing it to be the spot where Drake landed two centuries earlier.

1809 Russian captain Ivan Kuskov picks Bodega Bay as the port for a new Russian colony.

1812 Kuskov returns to California with 25 Russians and 80 Alaskan Natives to found Fort Ross. The

Feodor "Ted" Hahman, along with Barney Hoen, ran a trading company in the Carrillo adobe and in the early 1850s had the first business on Santa Rosa's new plaza. Courtesy, Healdsburg Museum

A leisurely day in front of the Wells-Fargo express office in Occidental. Occidental was a stop along the narrow gauge railroad between Marin and the Russian River. Courtesy, Sonoma County Historical Society

Alaskans in their baidarkas (kayaks) hunt the local sea otter population to near extinction for their pelts.

1817 Russians plant Sonoma County's first grapevines and apple orchards.

1823 Sonoma Mission, the last California Mission, founded by Father Altamira.

1833 Church turns the missions over to the Indians, few of whom end up with much land.

1835 Mariano Vallejo sent by Mexican government to establish a Northern Frontier to discourage Russian expansion; he gives ranchos of between 8,000 and 60,000 acres, many to his in-laws.

1836 Doña Maria Carrrillo founds first white settlement in Santa Rosa Plain.

1837 Smallpox epidemic brought by sailor kills hundreds of Native

Americans; many also die from European diseases like measles and cholera.

1841 Russians abandon Fort Ross. Pioneers from U.S. begin arriving.

1846 Distrust between Californios and American pioneers prompts Bear Flag Revolt two weeks before U.S. and Mexico go to war.

1848 Mexico cedes California to U.S. after its defeat in Mexican American War. Gold discovered in foothills of the Sierras, prompting temporary exodus from town of Sonoma.

1850 California becomes a state; Sonoma is named county seat.

1852 A.J. Cox starts the county's first newspaper, *Sonoma Bulletin*. Feodor Hahman, Barney Hoen and William Hartman survey and sell lots in Santa Rosa.

1854 County election makes Santa Rosa the new county seat.

1857 Harmon Heald sells parcels of his Sotoyome Rancho, setting aside land for a central plaza in the new town of Healdsburg. First steamer *Petaluma* begins run between Petaluma and San Francisco.

1859 Mendocino County created from the northern portion of Sonoma County. Squatters wars between newcomers and landowners at Bodega and Healdsburg.

1861 Agostin Haraszthy, founder of Buena Vista winery, returns from Europe with cuttings for 300 new varieties of wines, earning nickname "Father of California Viticulture."

1865 In one of the final actions of

Stone masons Peter Maroni (left) and August Deghi at the site of Santa Rosa's St. Rose church, 1900. Maroni, Deghi and others also built the four stone buildings at Railroad Square, including the 1908 railroad depot. Courtesy, Mike Capitani

the Civil War, hotheads from Petaluma ride towards Santa Rosa to chastise Southern sympathizers; they halt at Washoe Tavern and never fulfill their mission.

1875 Phylloxera, a vineyard pest, infests vines; growers forced to replant. Luther Burbank begins agricultural experiments. Thomas Lake Harris founds Fountaingrove colony.

1876 Narrow gauge rail line completed through west county to Russian River, prompting a boom in timbering and tourism.

1877 Broad gauge rail line from Santa Rosa to Russian River completed. Black Bart, the "PO8," robs the Duncans Mills stage, leaving a verse in the empty strongbox.

1879 Petaluman Lyman Byce perfects the chicken incubator.

1880 The Geysers are promoted as one of the wonders of the world, and throngs of tourists visit by stagecoach.

1881 Isaac DeTurk's wines win four firsts at State Fair. Andrea Sbarbaro founds Italian-Swiss Agricultural Colony in Asti.

1886 Anti-Chinese boycotts drive dozens of immigrants from the county.

1898 Petaluman Christopher Nisson perfects the incubator and founds Pioneer Hatchery, the first commercial hatchery in the U.S.

1906 Most of downtown Santa Rosa destroyed by earthquake.

1910 First Gravenstein Apple Fair in Sebastopol.

1911 Local pilot Fred Wiseman makes the world's first airmail flight, from Petaluma to Santa Rosa.

1918 Petaluma Chamber of Commerce promotes the town as the Egg Capital of the World. Santa

Rosa Junior College founded.

1920 Volstead Act (National Prohibition) deals major blow to county's 200 wineries. Three San Francisco gang members are lynched in Santa Rosa after they kill popular Sheriff Jim Petray.

1923 Major forest fire wipes out much of the remaining timber of the lower Russian River.

1925 Cecil B. DeMille films *Braveheart* in Guerneville, building an Indian village on the banks of the Russian River.

1930 End of narrow gauge rail service through Western Sonoma County.

1934 Founding of Sonoma Coast State Beaches.

1935 End of broad gauge rail service from Santa Rosa to Russian River. Prohibition repealed. Two labor leaders who organized apple pickers are tarred and feathered by vigilantes.

1936 First Sonoma County Fair.

1937 The Golden Gate Bridge, promoted by Santa Rosa Chamber of Commerce, opens. Ernest Finley, owner of the *Press Democrat*, founds radio station KSRO.

1938 Public Works Administration builds Analy Hall, Burbank Auditorium, and Bussman Hall on the Santa Rosa Junior College campus.

1941 At the start of World War II, infantry takes over Sonoma County fairgrounds; lookouts are placed on Mt. St. Helena and Mt. Jackson.

1942 758 Sonoma County residents of Japanese descent ordered

ABOVE: Sonoma's first Safeway store was next to B. Mori's store on West Napa Street. Courtesy, Sonoma Index-Tribune

BELOW: Fighter plane came to Fourth and Mendocino in downtown Santa Rosa to boost sales of war bonds, circa 1945. Courtesy, Sonoma County Museum

to leave their homes for internment camps. Alfred Hitchcock films *A Shadow of a Doubt* in Santa Rosa.

1946 Sonoma County Airport created from Santa Rosa Army Air Field.

1950 Hugh Codding kicks off building boom with 3,000 homes east of Santa Rosa.

1951 Rolf Illsley moves fledgling Optical Coating Labs, Inc. to Santa Rosa; OCLI paves way for other high-tech firms.

1961 Local residents thwart PG&E's plan to build a nuclear reactor on Bodega Head.

1962 John Glenn's orbiting space capsule has window coating from Optical Coating. Hitchcock films *The Birds* in Bodega and Bodega Bay. Rohnert Park incorporates.

1966 Sonoma State College moves to its own campus.

1967 Lou Gottlieb invites Haight-Ashbury folks to his Morning Star Ranch.

1968 Salt Point State Park founded.

1969 Twin earthquakes rock Santa Rosa, damaging downtown buildings including California Theatre and the Courthouse.

1971 5,000-acre Coney ranch becomes Annadel State Park.

1973 Descendants of founder Jacob Gundlach reopen the Gundlach-Bundschu Winery.

1974 Wine Road founded to promote Russian River Valley's wine regions.

1976 Christo Javacheff's Running Fence puts Sonoma County on the international art scene.

1979 Santa Rosa's 1910 post office is hauled from Fifth St. to Seventh St. to become the county's history museum.

1981 Luther Burbank Center for the Arts opens.

1982 The first Human Race fundraiser.

1983 Warm Springs Dam on Dry Creek west of Healdsburg creates Lake Sonoma reservoir to store water and curb flooding.

1984 County gets its own Public Broadcasting television station, KRCB/Channel 22.

1986 Major flood hits Russian River.

1992 Coast Miwok form tribal government under the name Federated Coast Miwok. Windsor incorporates.

1993 Sonoma County Historical Society sues City of Santa Rosa to block demolition of Rosenberg's store until a buyer is found.

1995 SRJC opens new campus in eastern Petaluma.

1996 Benziger Family winery in Glen Ellen plants county's first hops in decades.

1999 Vacu-dry, the second largest apple drying plant in the U.S., closes; Sonoma County—now recognized as one of the world's premier wine regions—has 45,000 acres of vineyards.

WORLD'S FIRST AIRMAIL

Fred J. Wiseman made history on February 17, 1911, when he took off from Petaluma's Kenilworth Park with three letters and 50 copies of the *Press Democrat*, which he dropped on subscribers along the way. After an unscheduled overnight stop in a muddy field, he landed his biplane the next morning just short of the Fairgrounds in Santa Rosa. The Smithsonian later confirmed his 14-mile jaunt as the world's first official airmail flight. Wiseman was a Santa Rosa race car driver who built his own plane after meeting the Wright Brothers in 1909. "I wonder how most of us were crazy enough to go up in the air in those kites we used to fly," he said 40 years later. "I must have been nuts." Ironically, by 1930 Wiseman had returned to a career in automotive engineering, convinced that aviation had a limited future. He died in 1961 at the age of 85. The plane now belongs to the Smithsonian. Courtesy, Sonoma County Museum.

Fred Wiseman (seated, with dog) and friends, including Grant Laughlin (second from left) and Bill Maddux (far right, with derby).

AVIATOR WISEMAN AND OFFICIALS ATTACHING A BAROGRAPH IMMEDIATELY BEFORE THE ENDURANCE RECORD TRIAL.

FRED J. WISEMAN
AVIATOR
SANTA ROSA, CAL.

Patrons

The following companies and organizations were invaluable to this publication. If not for them, this book would not have been possible. We gratefully acknowledge their participation in *Sonoma County: The River of Time.*

Balletto Ranch Inc.
Carlile • Macy
Hugh B. Codding
CrossCheck, Inc.
Dry Creek Vineyard
Eye Associates of Sebastopol

General Hydroponics, Inc.
Groskopf-Weider Trucking Co., Inc.
Hop Kiln Winery, Inc.
Komag Material Technology
Martini & Prati Winery
Max Machinery, Inc.
Monitor Publishing
Optical Coating Laboratory, Inc. (OCLI)
Pomeroy Corporation
Serres Corporation, Serres Ranch & Serres Vineyards
Sonoma County Museum
Stone Creek Wines
Weeks Drilling and Pump Company

Main Street U.S.A. has always been a focal point for the local residents of any community. This 1960s photo attests to this as locals of Santa Rosa socialize, shop, and take care of business along Santa Rosa's Fourth Street. The charm of Sonoma County has made it a favored setting for many successful films such as Peggy Sue Got Married, Goonies, American Graffiti, *and Alfred Hitchcock's* The Birds. *Courtesy, Sonoma County Museum*

Bibliography

Adams, Leon D. *The Wines of America*. New York: McGraw-Hill, 1978 and 1985.

Alexander, James B. *Sonoma Valley Legacy, Histories and Sites of 70 Historic Adobes*. Sonoma Valley Historical Society, 1986.

Alt, David D., and Donald W. Hyndman. *Roadside Geology of Northern California*. Missoula: Mountain Press Publishing, 1981.

Bailey, Floyd P. *Santa Rosa Junior College, 1918-1957: A Personal History*. Santa Rosa, 1967.

Bancroft, Hubert Howe. *History of California*, 7 vols. San Francisco: The History Company, 1886.

_____. *Register of Pioneer Inhabitants of California 1542 to 1848*. Baltimore: Regional Publishing, 1964.

Barrett, S.A. *Pomo Myths*. Milwaukee: Bulletin of the Public Museum of the City of Milwaukee, Vol. XV, 1933.

Bauer, Patricia M. "California's First Power Sawmill," *The Timberman*, September 1956.

Bean, Walton, and James J. Rawls. *California, an Interpretive History*. New York: McGraw-Hill, 1988.

Bell, Geoffrey. *The Golden Gate and the Silver Screen*. New York: Cornwall Books, 1984.

Benson, Foley. *From Straw into Gold; Selected Basketry Traditions of the American West*. Santa Rosa: Jesse Peter Memorial Museum, 1986.

Bidwell, John. *In California Before the Gold Rush*. Los Angeles: Ward Ritchie Press, 1948.

Bronstein, Zelda, and Kenneth Kann. "Basha Singerman, Comrade of Petaluma," *California Historical Society Quarterly*, Spring 1977.

Brown, Vinson and Douglas Andrews. *Pomo Indians of California and Their Neighbors*. Healdsburg: Naturegraph Publishers, 1969.

Bunje, Emil, and Frederick Schmitz. *Russian California 1805-1841*. Berkeley: U.S. Works Progress Administration, 1937.

Canillo, Alexis. *The Lonely Valley*. Santa Rosa Indian Center Heritage Project, 1980.

Carrillo, Alma McDaniel, and Eleanora Carrillo deHaney. *History and Memories: The Carrillo Family in Sonoma County*.

Clar, C. Raymond. *Out of the River Mist*. Santa Cruz: Forest History Society, 1973.

Cloverdale Then and Now. Cloverdale, 1982.

"The Coast Rangers: A Chronicle of Events in California," in *Harper's New Monthly Magazine*, July, 1861.

Cowan, G. Robert. *Ranchos of California, a List of Spanish Concessions 1775-1846*. Fresno: Academy Library Guild, 1956.

Cross, Ralph Herbert, *The Early Inns of California 1844-1869*. San Francisco: Cross and Brandt, 1954.

DeClerq, John H. *A History of Rohnert Park From Seed to City*. Rohnert Park, 1976.

DeTurk, Isaac. *Vineyards in Sonoma County*. Sacramento: Board of the State Viticultural Commission, 1893.

Dickinson, A. Bray. *Narrow Gauge to the Redwoods*. Trans-Anglo Books, 1970.

Dillon, Richard. *The Story of the Sea Ranch*. Oceanic Properties, 1965.

Dreyer, Peter. *A Gardener Touched with Genius: The Life of Luther Burbank*. Berkeley: University of California Press, 1985.

Duflot de Mofras, Eugene. *Travels on the Pacific Coast*. Santa Ana: Fine Arts Press, 1937.

Dutton, Joan Parry. *They Left Their Mark: Famous Passages through the Wine Country*. St. Helena: Illuminations Press, 1983.

Exploration du territoire de l'Oregon des Californies, et de la mer vermeille. Paris: Arthus Bertrand, 1844.

Finley, Ernest. *History of Sonoma County, California; Its People and Its Resources*. Santa Rosa: Press Democrat Publishing Co., 1937.

Gibson, James R. *Imperial Russia in Frontier America*. New York: Oxford University Press, 1976.

_____. "Russian Expansion in Siberia and America," in *Russia's American Colony*. S. Frederick Starr, ed. Durham: Duke University Press, 1987, pp. 32-40.

Golovnin, V.M. *Around the World on the Kamchatka, 1817-1819*. Honolulu: Hawaiian Historical Society, 1979.

Gregory, Tom. *History of Sonoma County, California with Biographical Sketches*. Los Angeles: Historic Record Co., 1911.

"The Gregson Memoirs," *California Historical Society Quarterly*, Vol. 19, 1940, pp. 113-143.

Handbook of North American Indians, Vol. 8. Robert F. Heizer, volume editor. Washington, D.C.: Smithsonian Institution, 1978.

Hanson, Harvey. *People on the Land; The Last Days of Fort Ross* (video).

_____, and Jeanne Thurlow Miller. *Wild Oats in Eden; Sonoma County in the 19th Century*. Santa Rosa, 1962.

Haraszthy, Agostin. *Father of California Wine: Agostin Haraszthy, with Grape Culture, Wines and Wine-Making*. Santa Barbara: Capra Press, 1979.

Heigh, Adair. *History of Petaluma, A California River Town*. Petaluma: Scottwall Associates, 1982.

Heizer, Robert F. *Elizabethan California*. Ramona, California: Ballena Press, 1974.

_____. *They Were Only Diggers; a Collection of Articles from California Newspapers 1851-1866, on Indian and White Relations*. Ramona, California: Ballena Press, 1974.

_____, and Albert B. Elsasser. *The Natural World of the California Indians*. Berkeley: University of California Press, 1980.

Hine, Robert V. *California's Utopian Colonies*. New York: W.W. Norman, 1966.

Hoffman, Ogden. *Reports of Land Cases Determined in the U.S. District Court for Northern District of California, 1852-1858*. Vol. I, 1862.

Ide, Simeon. *The Conquest of California: A Biography of William B. Ide*. Oakland: Biobooks, 1944.

Illustrated History of Sonoma County, California. Chicago: Lewis Publishing Co. 1889.

Interviews with Tom Smith & Maria Copa, Isabel Kelly's Ethnographic Notes on the Coast Miwok Indians of Marin and Southern Sonoma Counties, California. Compiled by Mary E.T. Collier and Sylvia B. Thalman. MAPOM Occasional Papers No. 6, San Rafael: Miwok Archaeological Preserve of Marin, 1996, 543 pp.

Jackson, Walter A. *Doghole Schooners*. Volcano, California: California Travelers, Inc., 1969.

Khlebnikov, Kyrill T. *Colonial Russian America, 1817-1832*. Portland: Oregon Historical Society, 1976.

Kneiss, Gilbert H. *Redwood Railways: A Story of the Redwoods, Picnic and Commuters*. Berkeley: Howell-North, 1956.

Kroeber, Alfred L. *Handbook of the Indians of California*. New York: Dover Publications, 1976 (reprint of Bureau of American Ethnology of the Smithsonian Institution, Bulletin 78, GPO, Washington, D.C., 1925).

Latimer, Patricia. *California Wineries, Vol.*

2: Sonoma and Mendocino. St. Helena: Vintage Image, 1976.

LeBaron, Gaye, and Dee Blackman, Joann Mitchell and Harvey Hansen. *Santa Rosa; A Nineteenth Century Town.* Santa Rosa: Historia, Ltd., 1985.

Lee, Hector. *Tales of California,* 1974.

MacMullen, Jerry. *Paddle-Wheel Days in California.* Palo Alto: Stanford University Press, 1944.

Marchand, Alexis. Unpublished letters to and from the Icarian community of Sonoma County. California Historical Society Library, San Francisco.

Margolin, Malcolm. *The Way We Lived; California Indian Reminiscences, Stories and Songs.* Berkeley: Heyday Books, 1981.

Marryat, Frank. N*orth Bay Journal and Visits to Gold Rush San Francisco.* Santa Rosa: Clio Publications, 1977 (reprint of 1855 first edition).

Mays, Verna. "Annadel; From Oak Woodland to Joe Coney's Dream Ranch to State Park," *Journal of the Sonoma County Historical Society,* 1994, No. 2, pp. 4-11.

McKee, Irving. "Historic Sonoma County Winegrowers," *California, The Magazine of the Pacific,* September 1955.

McKittrick, Myrtle M. *Vallejo, Son of California.* Portland: Binsford and Mort, 1944.

Mullen, Barbara Door. *Sonoma County Crossroads.* San Rafael, 1974.

Munro-Fraser, J.P. *History of Sonoma County, California, Illustrated.* Alley, Bowen & Co., 1880.

The New Shasta Daisies. Santa Rosa: Burbank's Experimental Farms, 1904.

New Historical Atlas of Sonoma County, Illustrated. Oakland: Thomas H. Thompson & Co., 1877.

Noto, Sal. "Homage to Jack London: The House of Happy Walls," *Pacific Historian,* Summer 1978.

O'Brien, Bickford, ed. *Fort Ross: Indians, Russians, Americans.* Jenner: Fort Ross Interpretive Association, 1980.

O'Brien, Robert. "The Passing of the Petaluma," *Riptides,* Aug. 30 and Sept. 1, 4 and 6, 1950.

Parmalee, Robert D. *Pioneer Sonoma.* Sonoma: Sonoma Index-Tribune, 1972.

Pastel, Consuelo M. *Loss of Property of the Japanese During World War II.* Sonoma State University, 1979.

Payeras, Fr. Mariano. *Travels of the Canon Fernandez de San Vincente to Ross.* Nicholas Del Cioppo, ed. and translator. Aug. 1979. Bancroft Manuscript Collection MS C-C18, pp. 411-428.

Pelanconi, Joseph D. *Quicksilver Rush of Sonoma County, 1873-75.* Chico State College M.A. thesis, 1969.

Perez, Cris. *Grants of Land in California Made by Spanish or Mexican Authorities.* State Lands Commission.

Phillips, Linda. *Impact of Rail Transportation on Urban Geography of Santa Rosa, California 1854-1906.* Sonoma State University M.A. thesis, 1986.

Reed, Anna M. "Prohibition Is Piracy," *Northern Crown,* Petaluma, 1916.

Report to Mariano G. Vallejo: Confidential Information Concerning the Ross Settlement, 1833. Nicholas Del Cioppo, ed. and translator, California Dept. of Recreation and Parks, Aug. 1979.

Robinson, W.W. *Land in California.* Berkeley: University of California Press, 1948.

Roddy, W. Lee. *Black Bart and Other California Outlaws,* 1970.

Rolle, Andrew, "Italians in California," *Pacific Spectator,* Autumn 1955.

Sail and Steam on the Northern California Coast 1850-1900. Compiled by Wallace E. Martin. San Francisco: National Maritime Museum Association, 1983.

Schubert, John C. *Guerneville Early Days, A History of the Lower Russian River.* Guerneville, 1997.

Shutes, Milton. "Fightin' Joe Hooker," *California Historical Society Quarterly,* 1937, pp. 304-320.

Smith, Barbara Sweetland, and Redwood J. Barnett. *Russian America: The Forgotten Frontier.* Tacoma: Washington State Historical Society, 1990.

Smith, John Stephen. *Sonoma County Exiles: The Japanese-Americans and World War II.* Sonoma State University, 1975.

Speth, Frank Anthony. *A History of Agricultural Labor in Sonoma County, California.* University of California M.A. thesis, 1938.

Stevenson, Robert Louis. *The Silverado Squatters.* San Francisco: Grabhorn Press, 1952 (reprint of 1883 edition).

Stindt, Fred A. *Trains to the Russian River,* 1974.

Tays, George. "Mariano Guadalupe Vallejo and Sonoma," *California Historical Quarterly* Vol. 16, pp. 99-121, 216-55 and 348-72; Vol. 17, pp. 50-73, 141-67 and 219-42.

Thalman, Sylvia B. *The Coast Miwok Indians of the Point Reyes Area.* Point Reyes National Seashore Association, 41 pp.

Thompson, Robert A. *Conquest of California.* Santa Rosa: Sonoma Democrat Publishing Co., 1896.

_____ . *Historical and Descriptive Sketch of Sonoma County, California.* Philadelphia: L.H. Everts & Co., 1877.

Truffaut, François. *Hitchcock.* New York: Simon and Schuster, 1967.

Trussell, Margaret E. *Settlement of the Bodega Bay Region.* University of California M.A. thesis, 1960.

Tuomey, Honoria. *History of Sonoma County, California,* 2 vols. Chicago: S.J. Clarke, 1926.

U.S. Works Progress Administration. *Sonoma County History and Description.* Compiled by Dorothy Wolf, Richard Brooks and Albert A. Pond. Santa Rosa, 1936.

_____ . *Foreign Born in Sonoma County.* Compiled by Richard Brooks and Dorothy Wolf. Santa Rosa, 1936.

We Are Still Here—A Coast Miwok Exhibit, catalogue of an exhibit at Bolinas Museum, 1993, with an introduction by Greg Sarris, 17 pp.

Willson, Carolyn. "London Album: A California Legend at Work and Play," *California Historical Quarterly,* Fall 1976.

Wilson, Simone. "Lights, Camera, Action! — Sonoma County in the Movies," *Journal of the Sonoma County Historical Society,* 1994, No. 3, pp. 4-10.

_____ . "Prime Suspect — Sensational 1880's Murder Inflames Anti-Immigrant Hysteria," *Albion Monitor,* Sept. 29, 1996 (reprinted in *Journal of Sonoma County Historical Society,* 1996, No. 4, pp. 12-15).

The World Encompassed by Sir Francis Drake, carefully collected out of the notes of Master Francis Fletcher. London: printed for Nicholas bourne, 1628.

Index

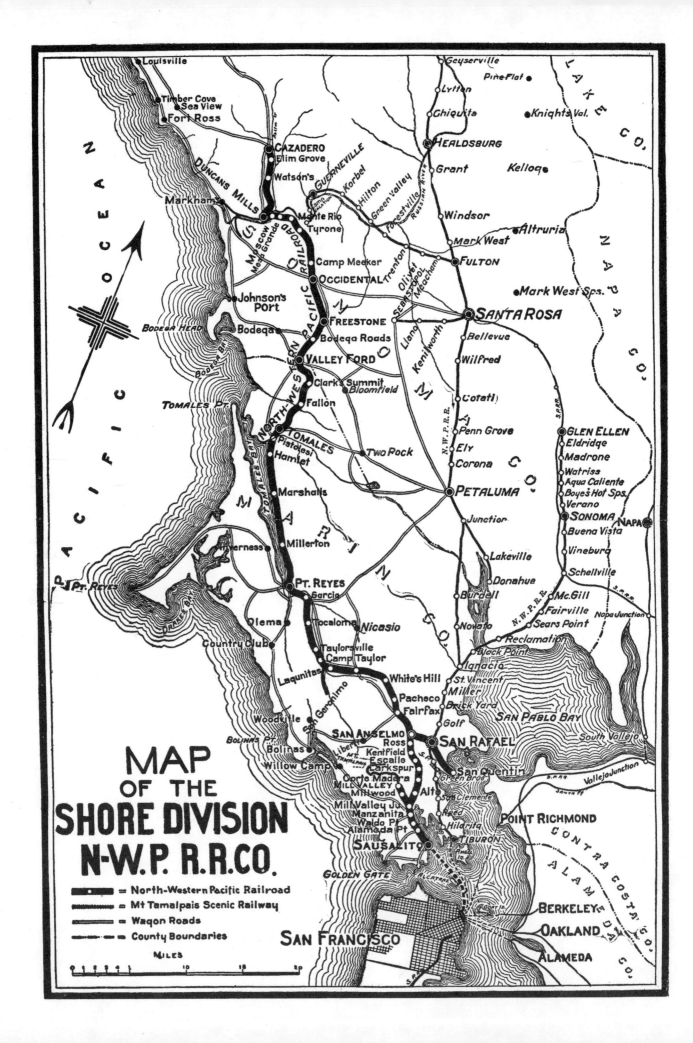

MAP
OF THE
SHORE DIVISION
N-W.P. R.R.CO.

MILES

●━━━● = North-Western Pacific Railroad
━━━━━ = Mt Tamalpais Scenic Railway
━━━━━ = Wagon Roads
━━━━━ = County Boundaries